HOT BLUES GUITAR #2

Authentic Tablature Transcriptions Off the Original Recordings
Transcribed by Billy Simms

Contents

Produced by John L. Haag

Catalog # 07-4039
ISBN# 1-56922-031-X

Exclusive Distributor:
CREATIVE CONCEPTS PUBLISHING CORPORATION, 410 Bryant Circle, Box 848, Ojai, CA 93024

STEVIE RAY VAUGHAN

CLARENCE "GATEMOUTH" BROWN

HOWLIN' WOLF

MUDDY WATERS

JOHNNY "GUITAR" WATSON

OTIS RUSH

LONNIE MACK

FREDDIE KING

B. B. KING

EDDIE KIRKLAND

JIMMY REED

ELMORE JAMES

BILL WITHERS

LIGHTININ' HOPKINS

EARL HOOKER

BUDDY GUY

ALBERT KING

LOWELL FOLSUM

JOHNNY COPELAND

ALBERT COLLINS

GEORGE THOROGOOD

ERIC CLAPTON

ROBERT CRAY

JOHNNY COPELAND, ROBERT CRAY & ALBERT COLLINS

THE FABULOUS THUNDERBIRDS

THE NOTATION

Each guitar part is written in both musical notation and guitar tablature.

The tablature tells you which strings should be played at which frets. The six lines of the staff correspond to the strings of the guitar, first string at the top, and the numbers written on the lines indicate which frets should be fingered.

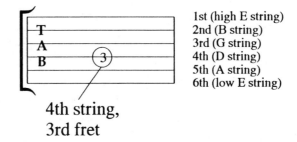

1st (high E string)
2nd (B string)
3rd (G string)
4th (D string)
5th (A string)
6th (low E string)

4th string,
3rd fret

The numbers in the tablature staff should be played with the same rhythm that is written in the music notation staff. (if you're unfamiliar with musical notation, the best plan is to listen to and play along with the recording of the song.) Numbers that are stacked on top of one another should be fingered and played simultaneously as a chord.

Left hand fingering has not been indicated. If you play through a line two or three times, the correct (that is, easiest) fingering should become apparent.

Blues is repetitive: that's part of its charm. There are symbols used throughout to indicate repeating the previous measure, or the previous two measures.

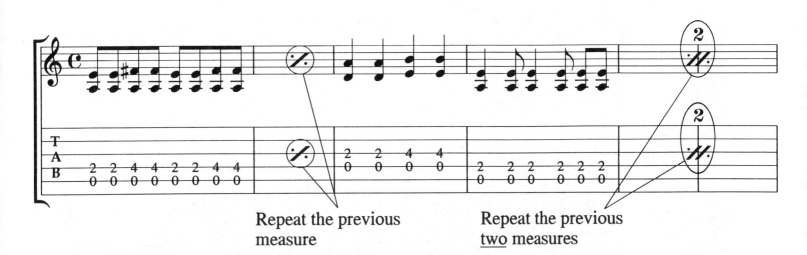

Repeat the previous
measure

Repeat the previous
two measures

Here is the tablature for some common guitar technique:

<u>BENDS</u> - Finger the string at the fret shown and bend it upwards to
produce the note that would ordinarily be heard at the fret
number in parenthesis. This usually occurs on the first three
strings. Pre-bends are notated in tablature and musical notation
in the same manner as the standard bend , however they are indicated
with the word "pre-bend". In the case of pre-bends, the string
is bent before the string is struck. Quarter ($\frac{1}{4}$) bends are
indicated in both musical notation and tablature as an upward
slur above the note / fret.

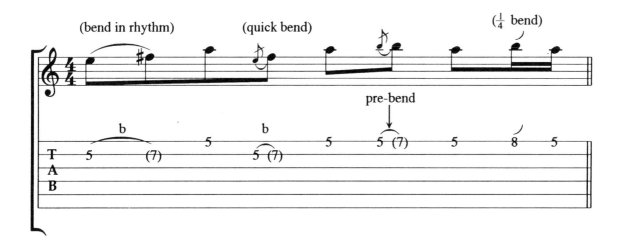

Unless otherwise paired with slurs or footnotes, parenthetic
fret numbers / notes indicate"ghost-notes"- very faint pitches
produced either with left or right hand.

<u>HAMMER-ONS</u> - Finger the string at the fret shown and produce the next note not by picking it
with the right hand, but by hammering a finger of your left hand onto the indicated fret.

PULL-OFFS - Finger the string simultaneously at the fret shown and at the next fret shown. Pick the first note, and produce the next note by plucking the string with the left-hand finger you're pulling off.

SLIDES - Finger the string at the fret shown and, without lifting your finger, slide up or down to the next indicated fret.

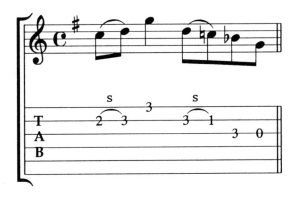

If no fret number is shown before the slide, start a fret or two away and slide quickly to the indicated fret. Or slide away from the indicated fret to an undetermined fret, lifting your finger as you go to mute the string.

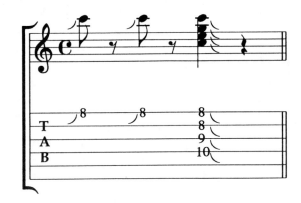

Any of these slides can be performed on single strings or with whole chords.

BLACK CAT BONE

Transcribed Off The Recording by Albert Collins, Robert Cray and Johnny Copeland on the Alligator CD "Showdown!"

Guitar Tablature Transcription
by
Billy Simms

Words and Music by
Harding "Hop" Wilson

Guitar 1: (Albert Collins) Fm Tuning

⑥ = F   ④ = F   ② = C
⑤ = C   ③ = Ab   ① = F

Guitar 2: (Johnny Copeland) Standard Tuning

⑥ = E   ④ = D   ② = B
⑤ = A   ③ = G   ① = E

Medium Rock Groove

(band enters) **C7**

4 X

8 measures of Dialogue between
Albert Collins and Johnny Copeland   4th X only   1.I be-

Gtr 1. Albert Collins   Capo a 7th fret

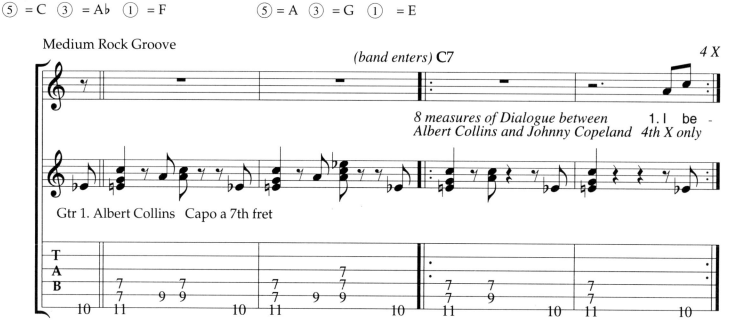

A

lieve. _____   My   ba-by got a black cat bone.   Oh, yeah,   yeah   I be-lieve

A.C.---------

Gtr. 1

Gtr. 2 Johnny Copeland

My ba-by got a black cat bone.

Seem like e-

(e)- very-thing I do, seem like I do it wrong

Well you see I tried _ so hard _ to get a - long _ with that wo-man

Gtr. 2 continue rhythmic figure A

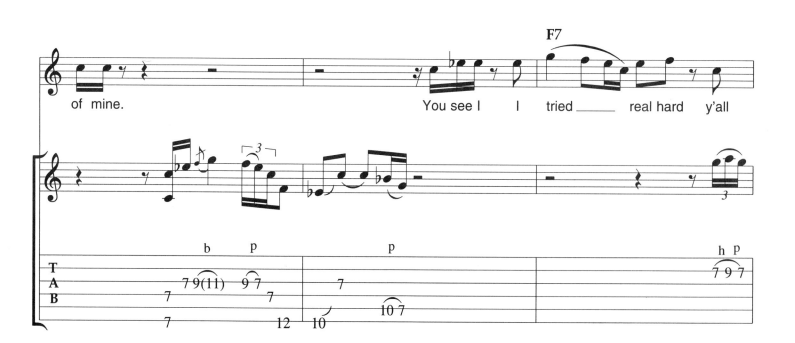

of mine. You see I I tried real hard y'all

walked down from Dallas, Texas   down to Wichita   Falls. I got to thin-kin' a-bout the big-legged wo-man   and

Gtr. 2

went down wal-kin' on.   I be-lieve_____   my ba-by got a black cat

_ bone.

look like e - very-thing I do

e-very-thing I do _ is wrong. _ Ha!   Play it Al-bert.

Solo(Albert Collins)

Gtr. 2 rhythmic pattern A

Solo (Johnny Copeland)

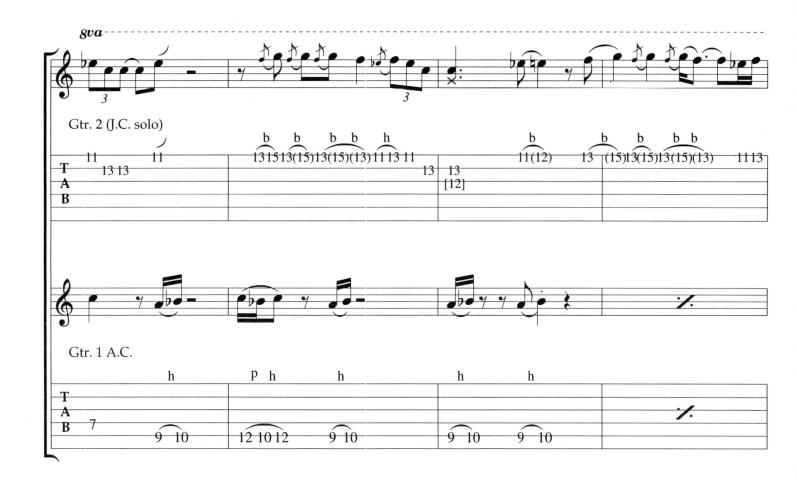

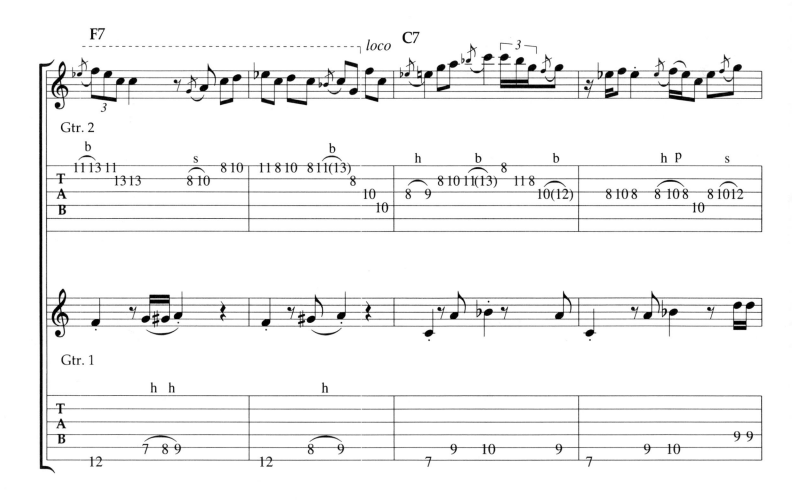

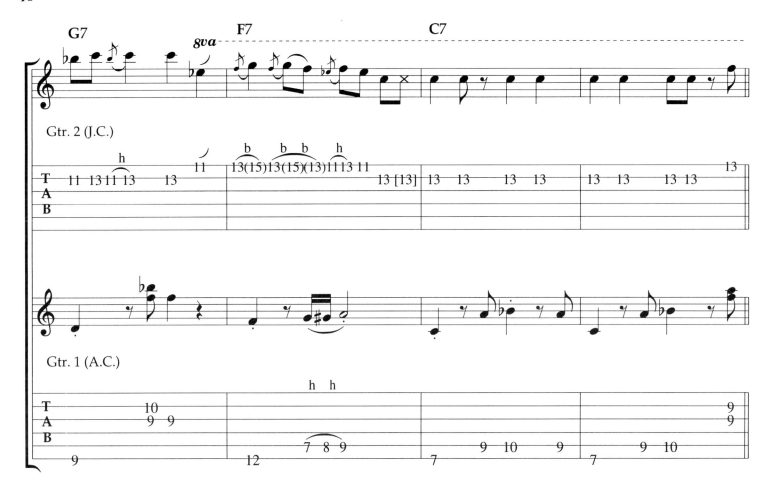

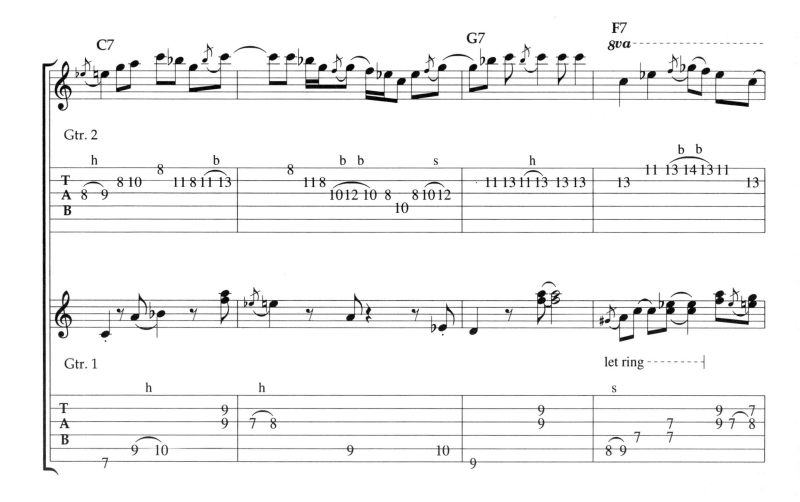

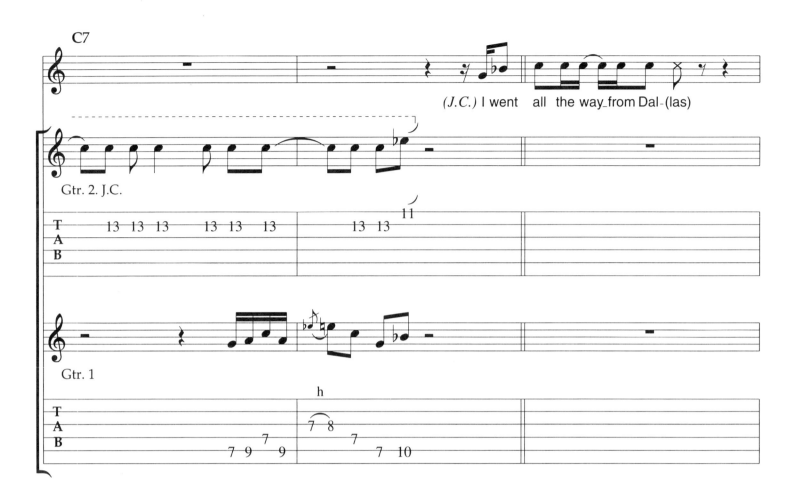

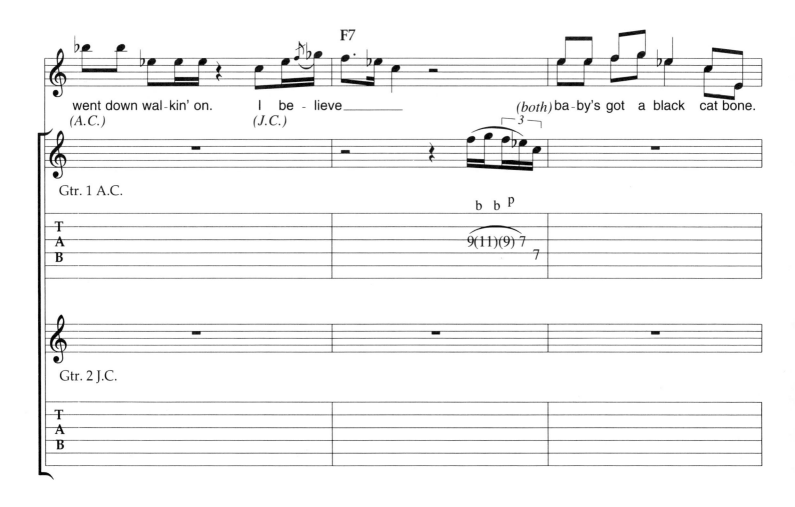

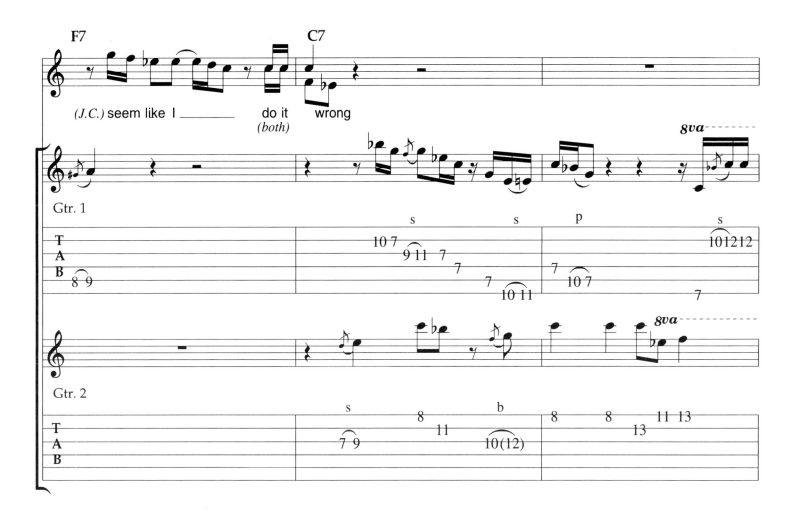

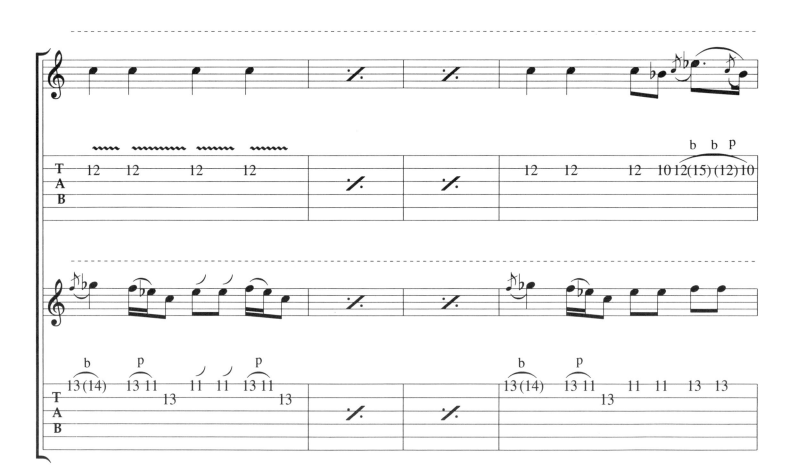

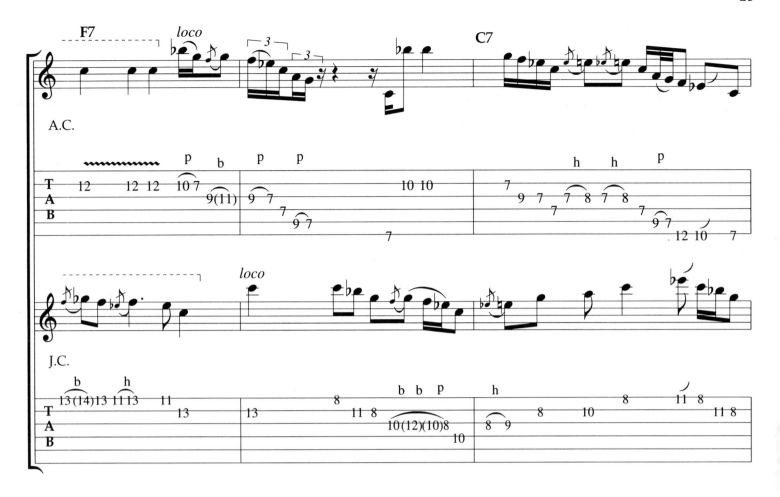

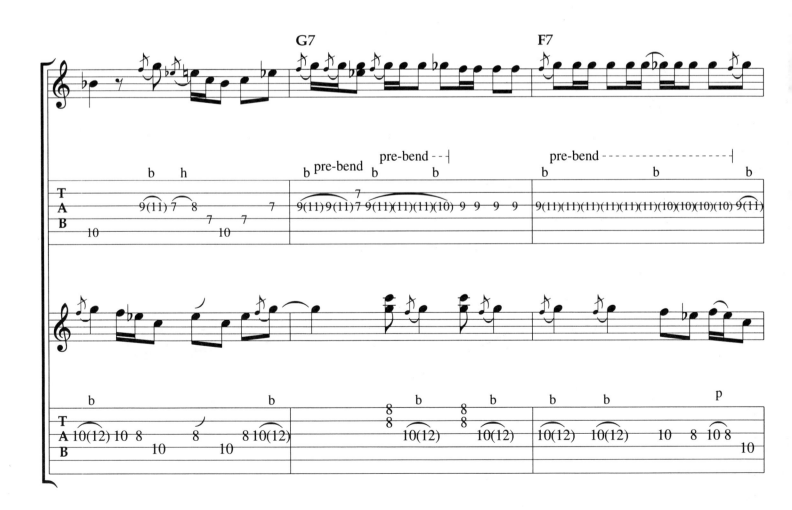

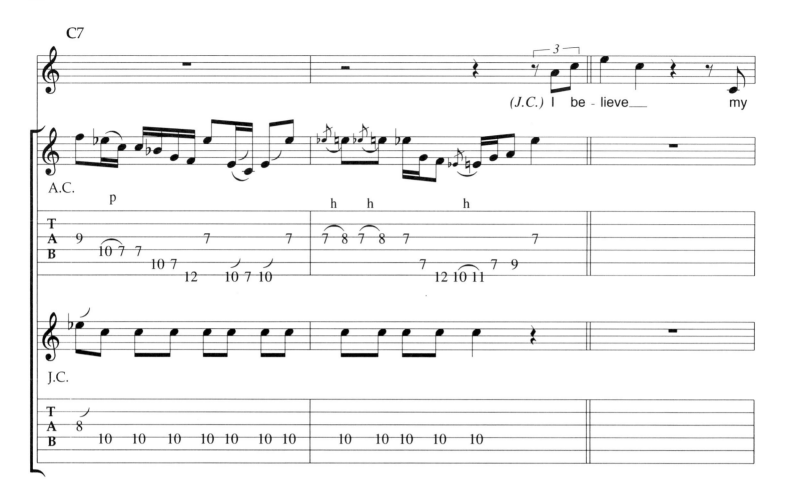

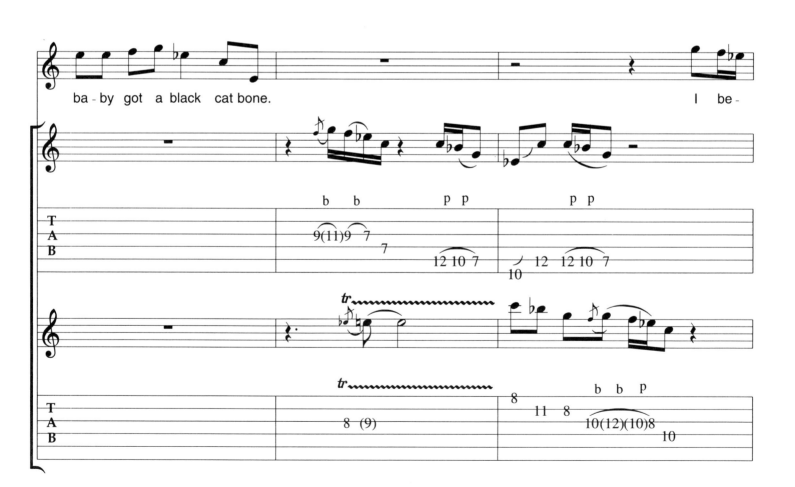

lieve _____ my ba - by got a black cat bone.

Seems like e - (e) - very-thing I do ___ seem like I ____ do it wrong

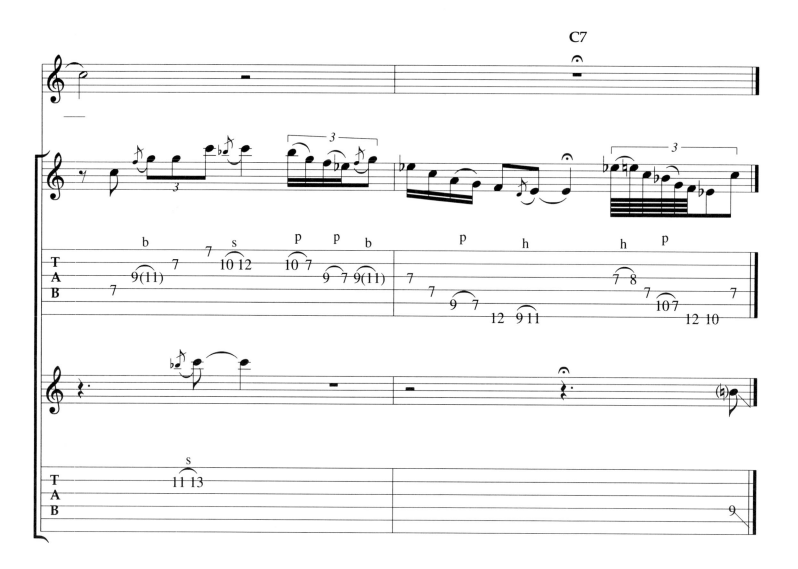

BACK DOOR FRIEND

Transcribed Off The Album "Blue Lightnin"

Guitar Tablature Transcription
by
Richard De Vinck

Words and Music by
Stan Lewis and Lightnin' Sam Hopkins

Standard Tuning:

⑥ = E ④ = D ② = B
⑤ = A ③ = G ① = E

Moderately Slow Blues Shuffle

Triplet Feel

* C♮ unintentional
note

Slight mute on low E stg.

* Let ring into next bar

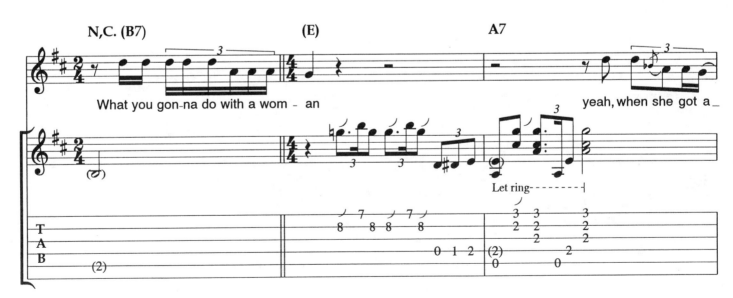

What you gon-na do with a wom - an

yeah, when she got a_

Let ring--------

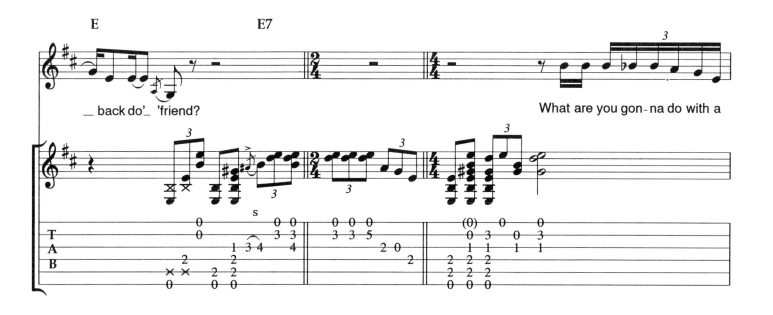

back do' 'friend?

What are you gon- na do with a

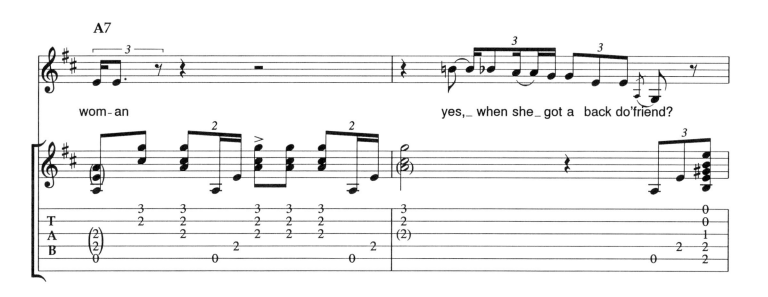

wom- an

yes,_ when she_ got a back do'friend?

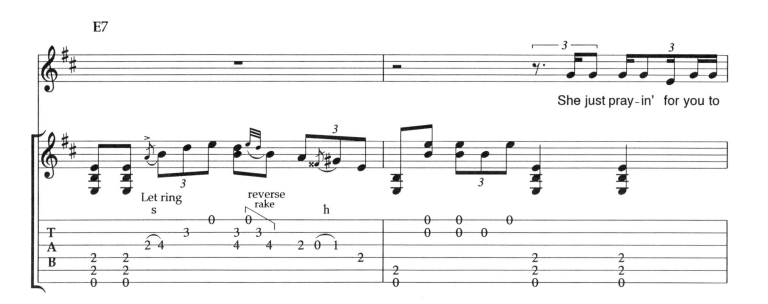

She just pray- in' for you to

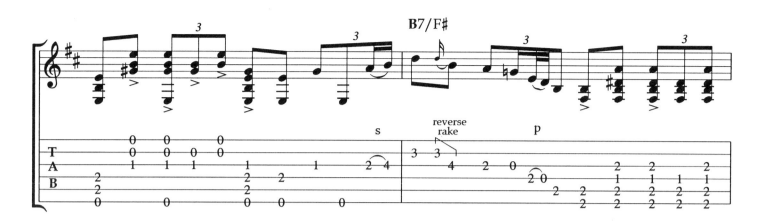

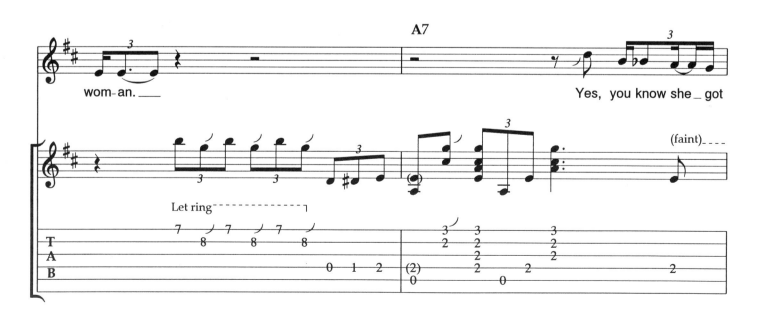

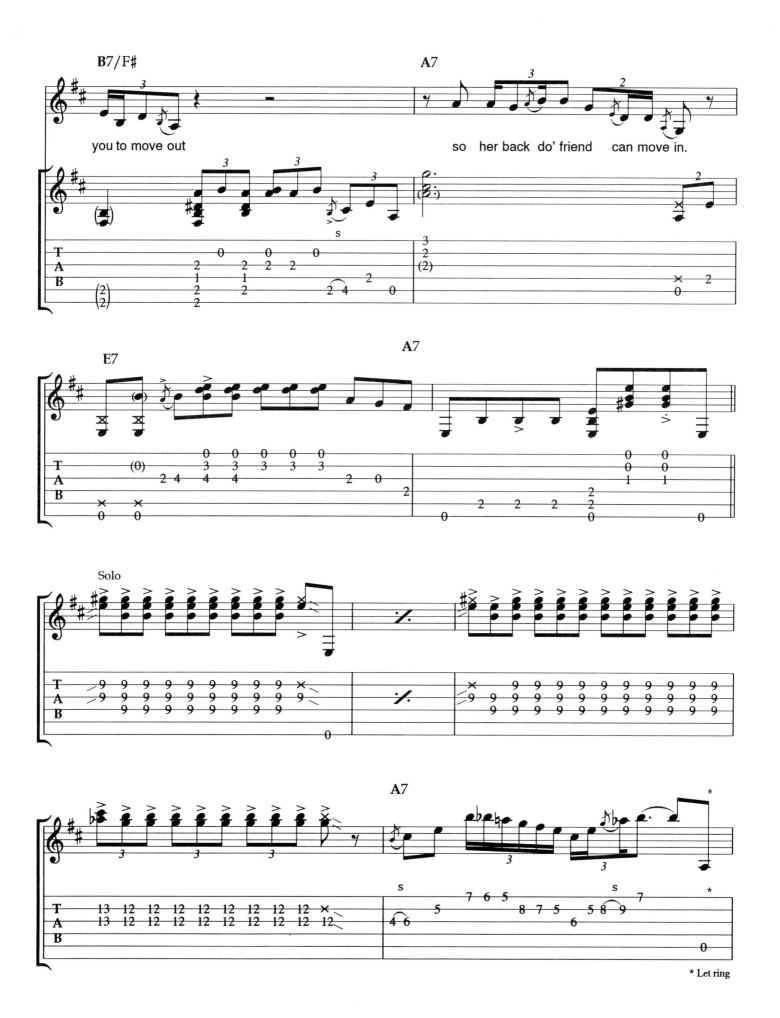

you to move out

so her back do' friend can move in.

Solo

* Let ring

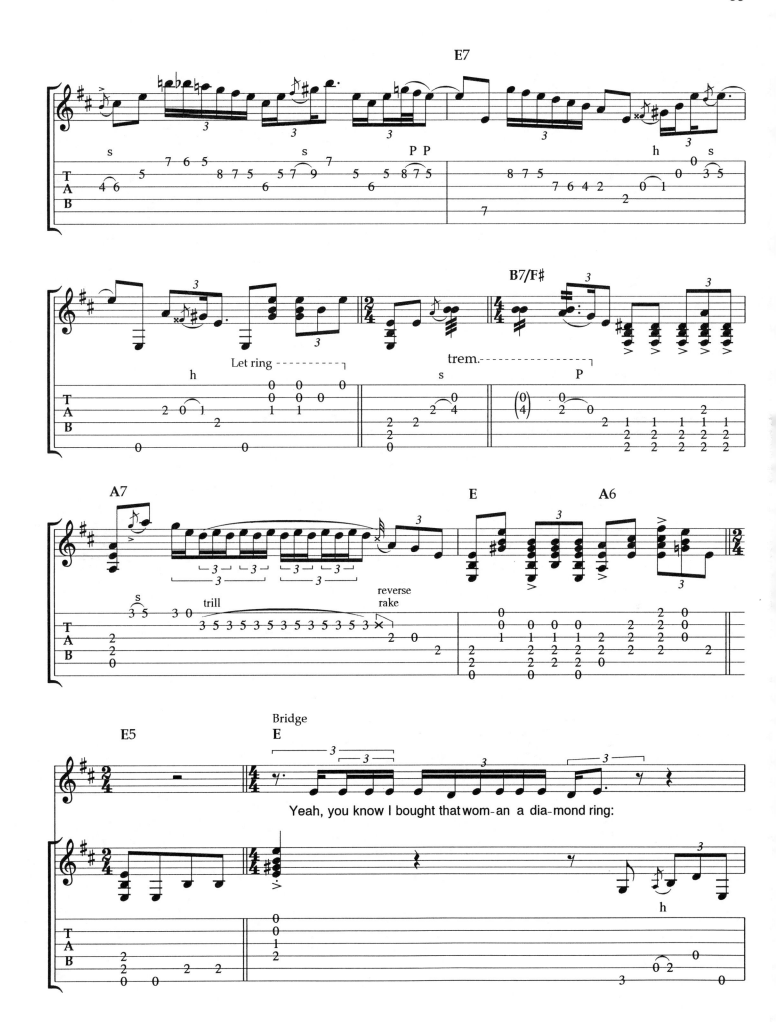

Yeah, you know I bought that wom-an a dia-mond ring:

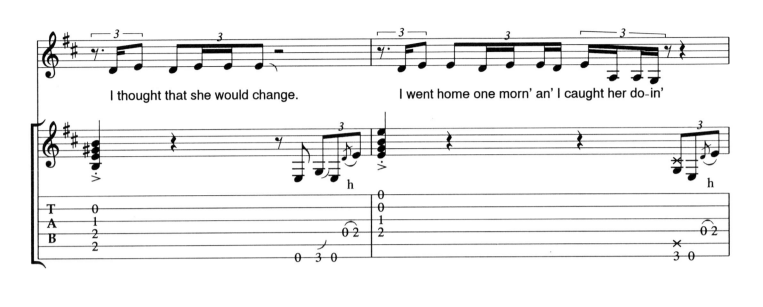

I thought that she would change.   I went home one morn' an' I caught her do-in'

whoa, that same old thing.__ Now what you gon' do with a mad wom-an

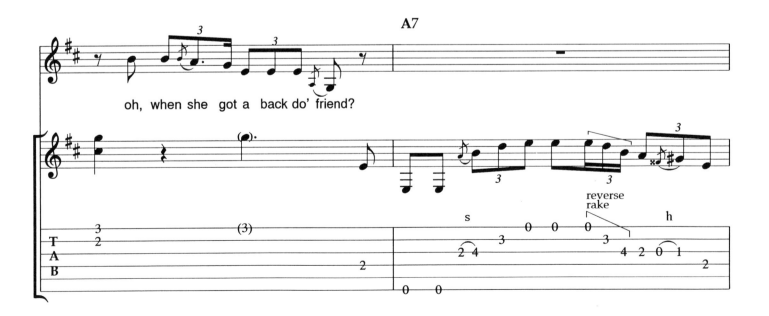

oh, when she got a back do' friend?

When she pray in' all the time   for you to move out_

so her_ back do'_ friend, he can move in.

AIN'T NO SUNSHINE

Transcribed Off The Recording by Freddie King on the Shelter/DCC CD "Freddie King - The Texas Cannonball"

Guitar Tablature Transcription
by
Billy Simms

Words and Music by
Bill Withers

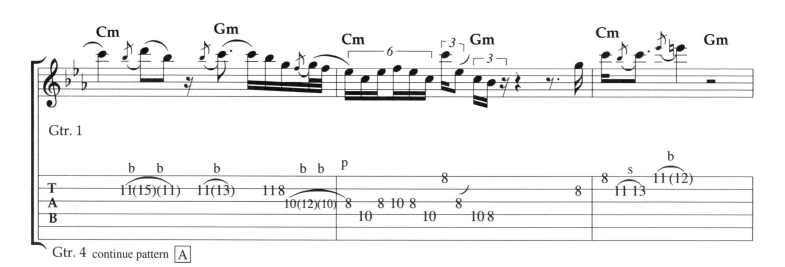

Gtr. 4 continue pattern [A]

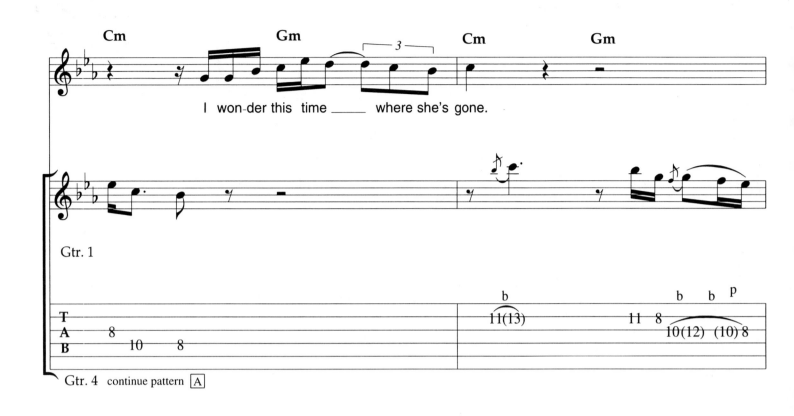

Gtr. 1

Gtr. 4   continue pattern A

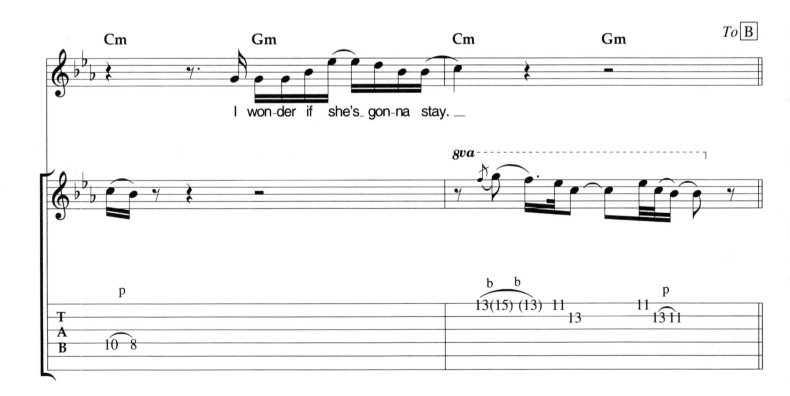

Solo Break

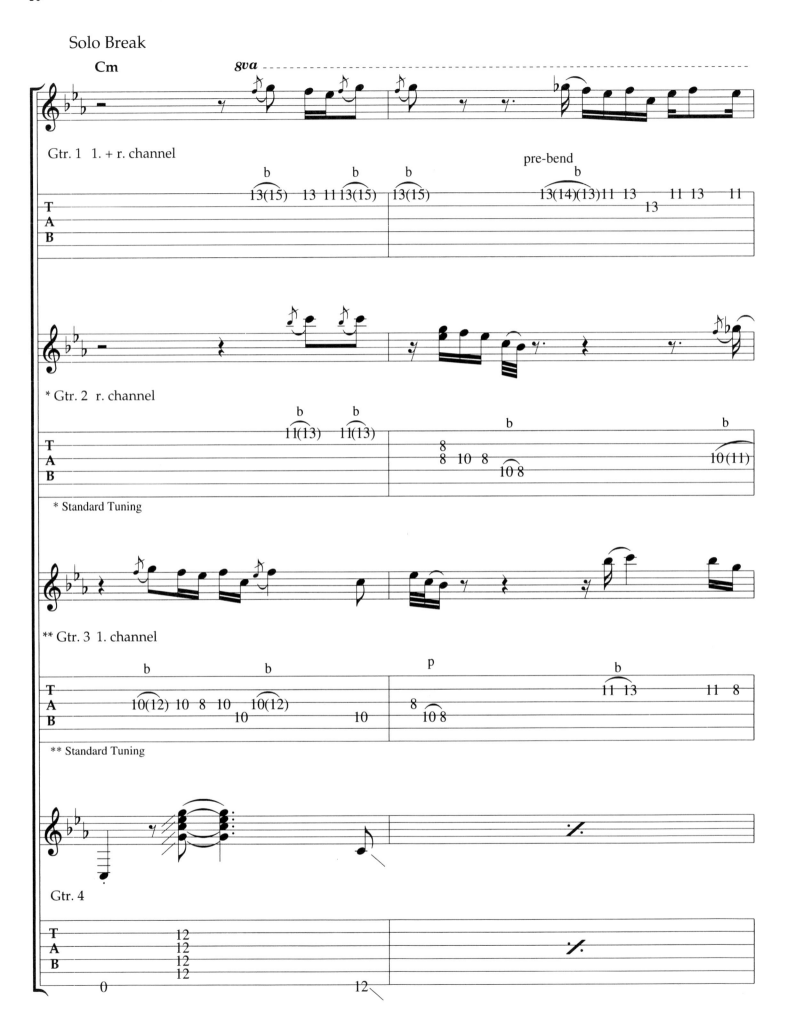

Well _ I got a lit-tle young thing a-lone. Ain't no sun - shine when she's

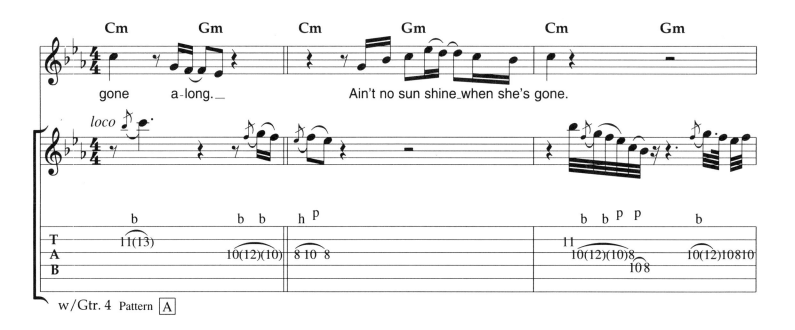

w/Gtr. 4 Pattern A

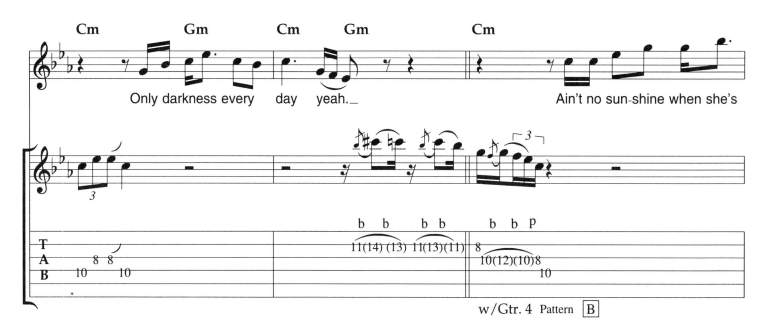

w/Gtr. 4 Pattern B

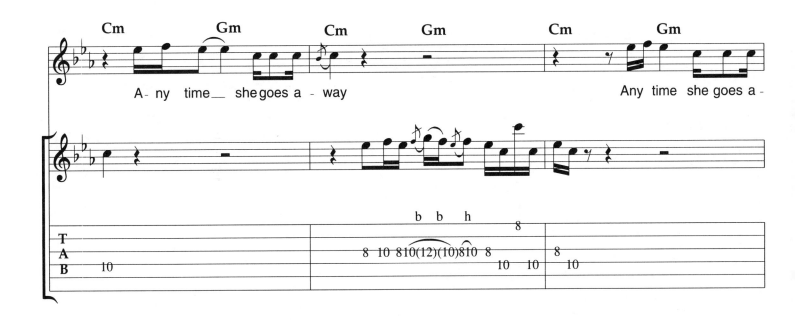

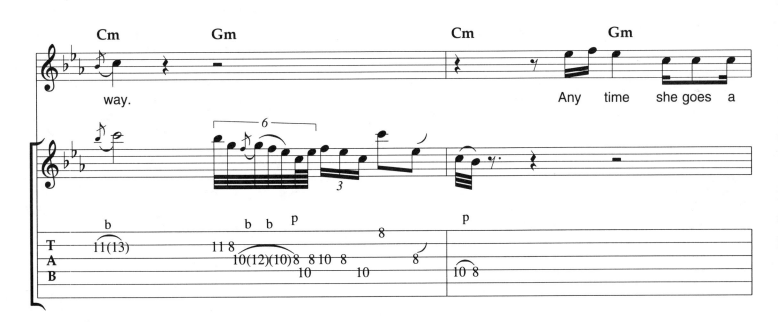

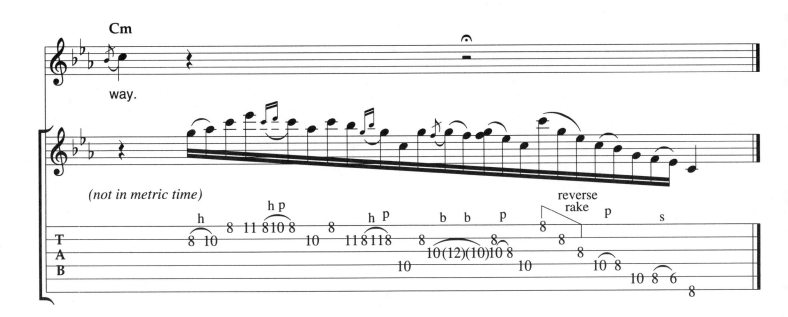

BAD LUCK SOUL

Transcribed Off The Recording by B. B. King on the Flair/Virgin CD "The Best Of B. B. King Vol. 2"

Guitar Tablature Transcription
by
Billy Simms

Words and Music by
Riley B. King and Jules Taub

Standard Tuning:

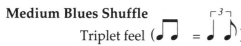

⑥ = E   ④ = D   ② = B
⑤ = A   ③ = G   ① = E

Medium Blues Shuffle

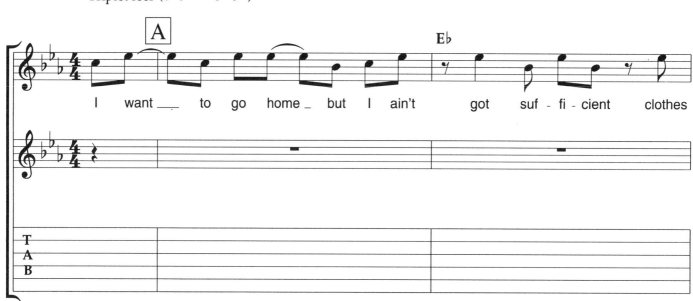

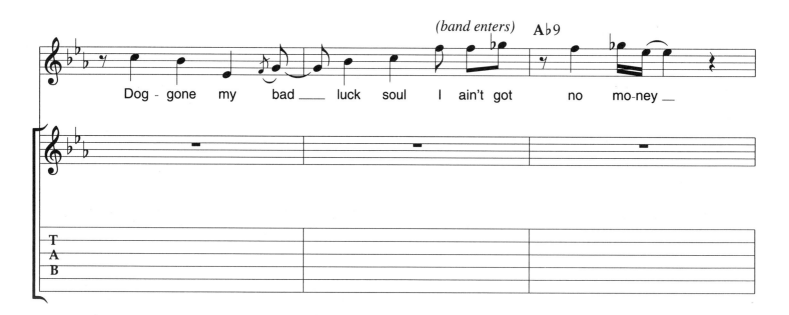

47

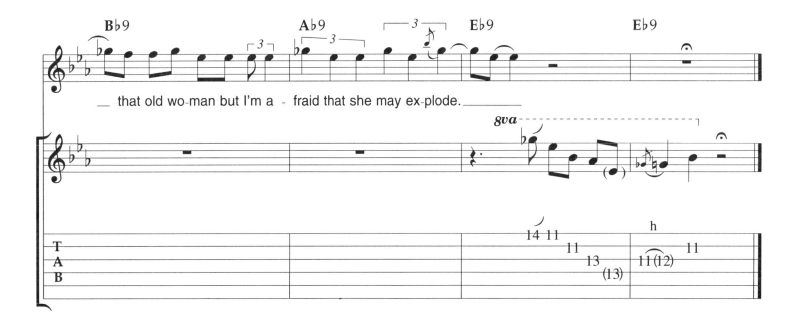

Additional Lyrics

2. My wife done quit me, my girlfriend too.
   Dog gone my bad luck soul.
   I ain't got nobody and I don't know what to do.
   They say things will get better, but I don't believe it's true.

3. I thought I had friends but they all disappeared.
   Dog-gone my bad luck soul.
   Everything I do people everything I do seems to be wrong.
   It wouldn't be so bad if I knew that I had a home.

HOT LITTLE MAMA

Transcribed Off The Recording by Johnny "Guitar" Watson on the Flair/Virgin CD "Three Hours Past Midnight"

Guitar Tablature Transcription
by
Billy Simms

Words and Music by
Johnny "Guitar" Watson,
Maxwell Davis and Jules Taub

Standard Tuning:

⑥ = E ④ = D ② = B
⑤ = A ③ = G ① = E

Medium Blues Shuffle

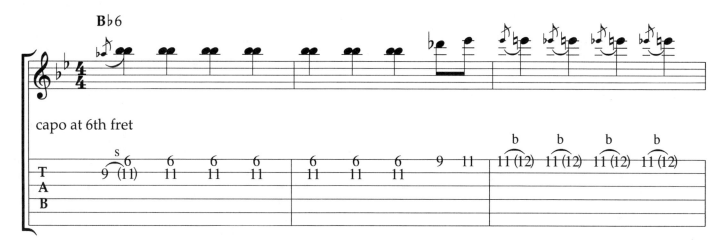

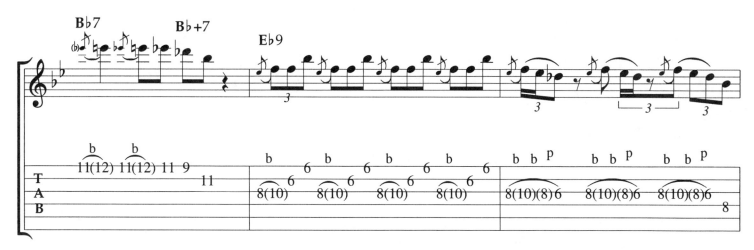

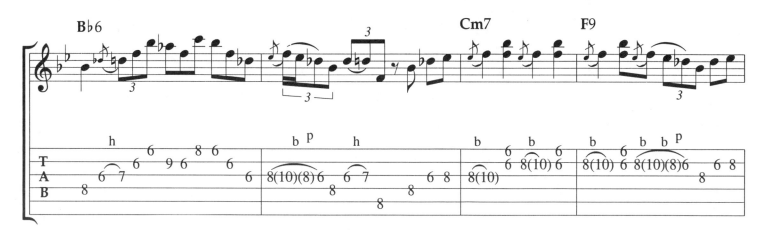

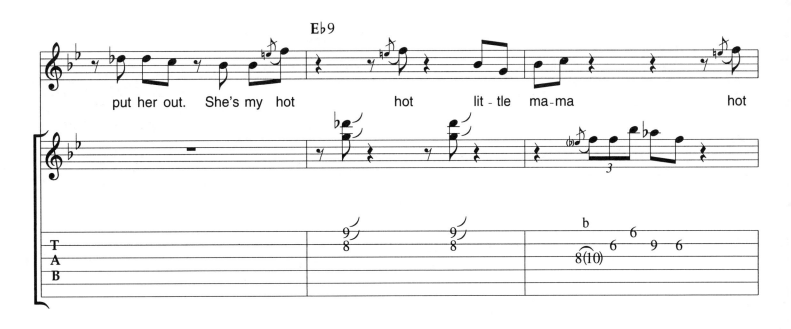

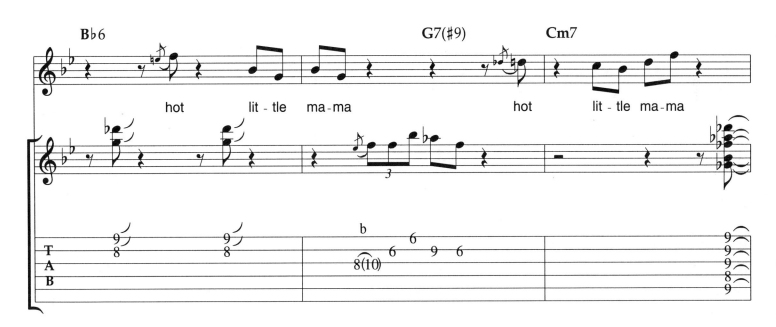

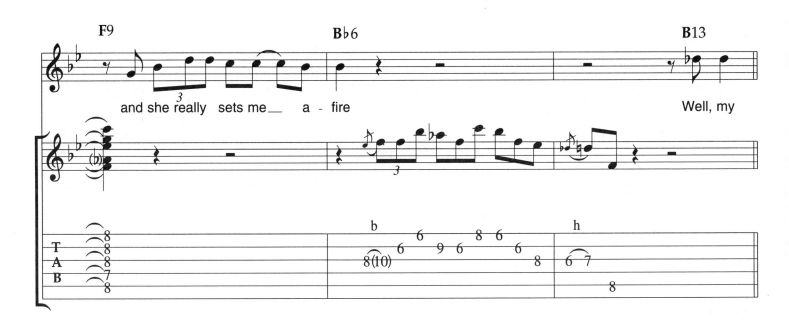

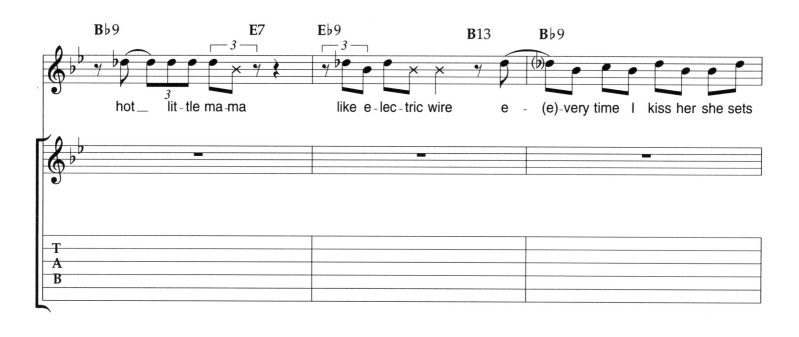

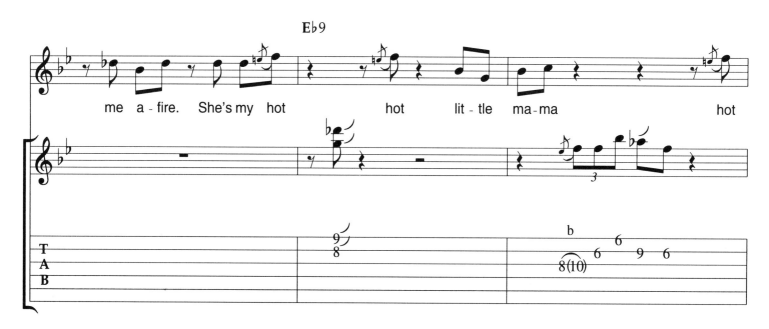

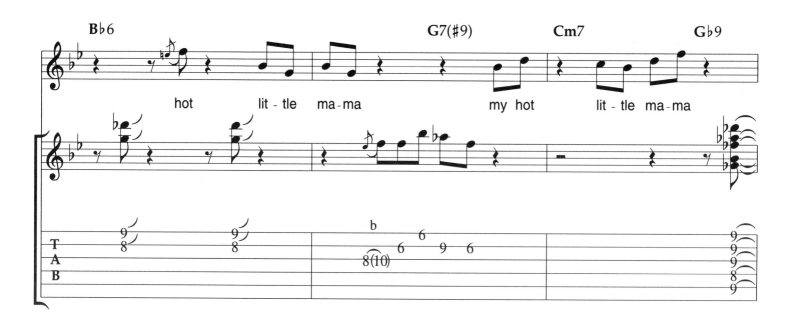

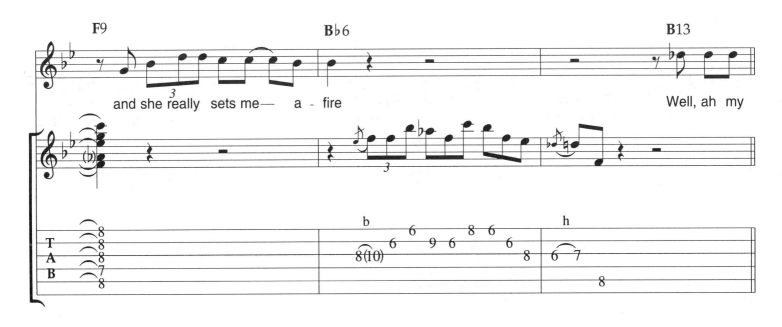

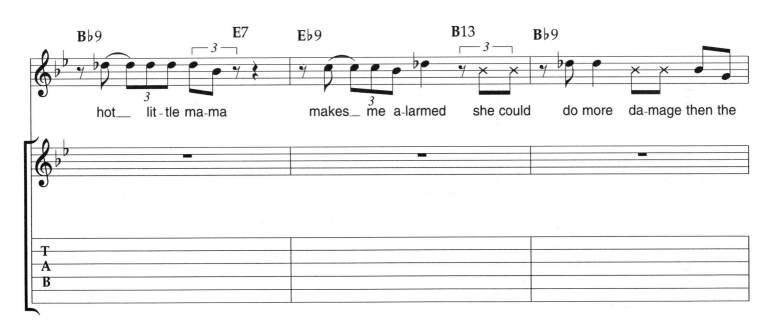

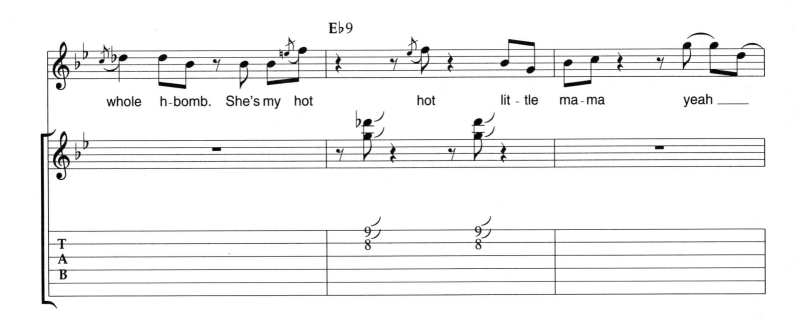

56

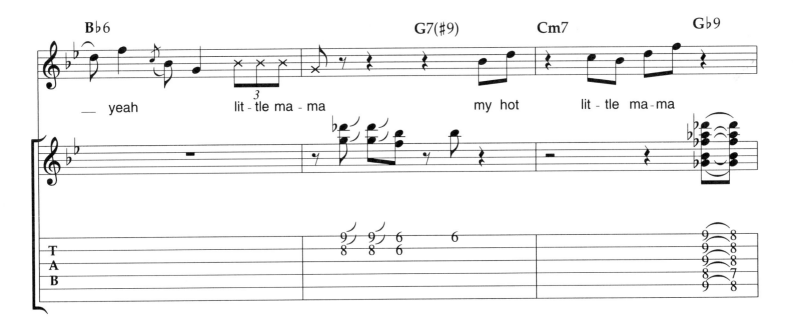

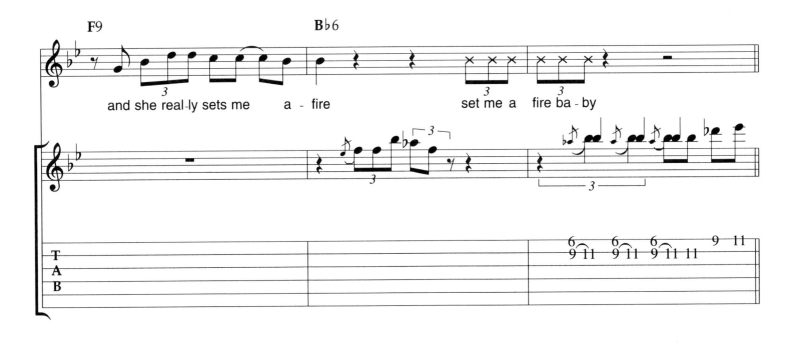

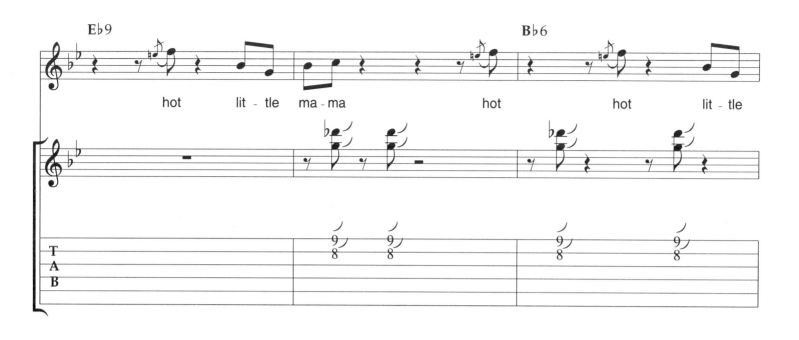

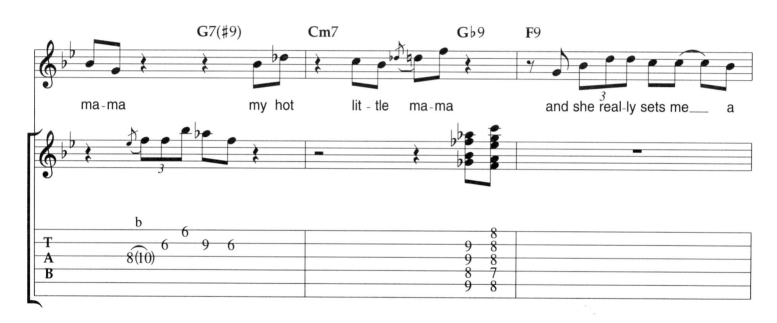

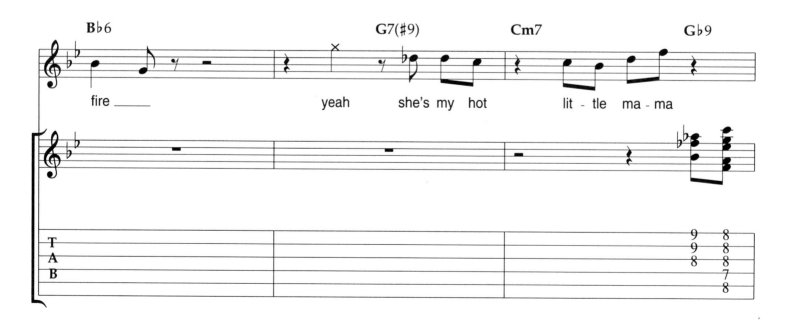

and she real-ly sets me a - fire

CAMP WASHINGTON CHILI

Transcribed Off The Album "Lonnie Mack : Second Sight"

Guitar Tablature Transcription
by
Richard De Vinck

Music by
Lonnie Mack, Tim Drummond,
and Stan Szelest

Tune Up 1/2 Step:

⑥ = F ④ = E♭ ② = C
⑤ = B♭ ③ = A♭ ① = F

Moderately Fast Blues Instrumental

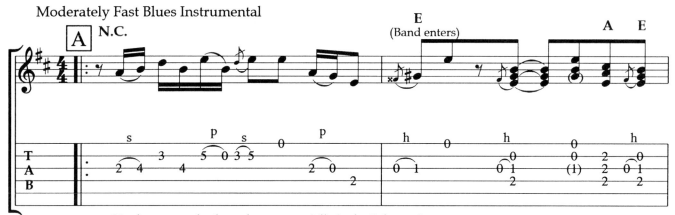

Use heavy attacks throughout - especially in the Solo sections.

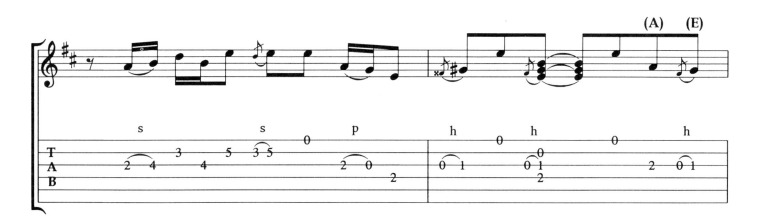

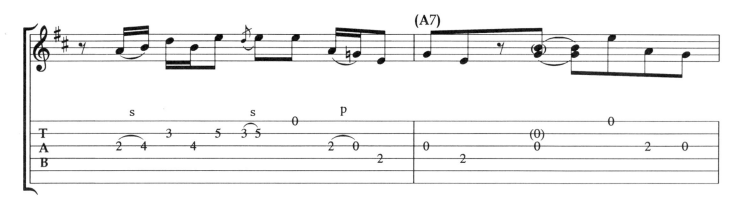

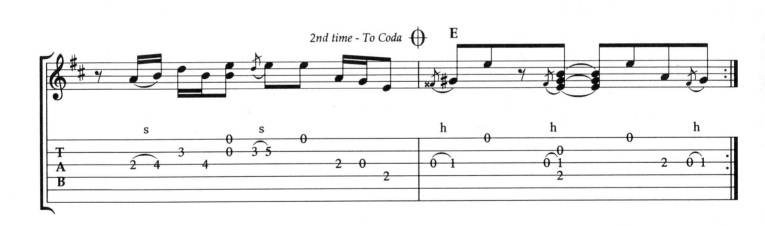

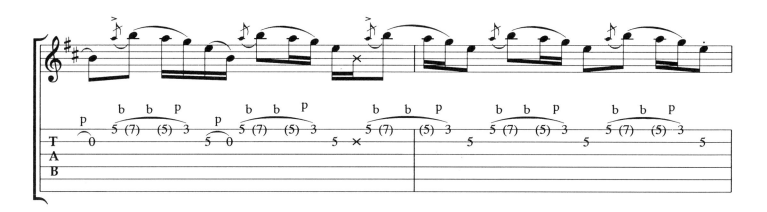

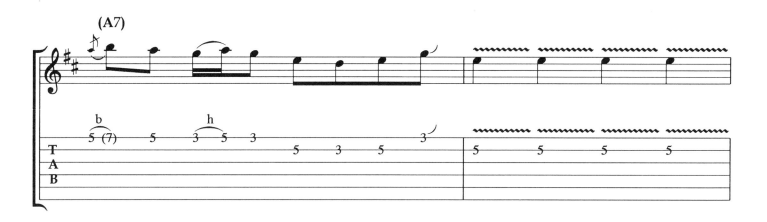

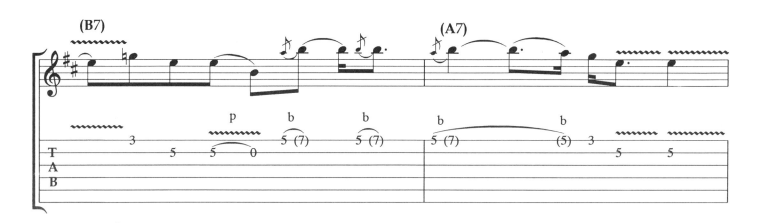

Half - Time w/Swing Feel (♫ = ♩♪)

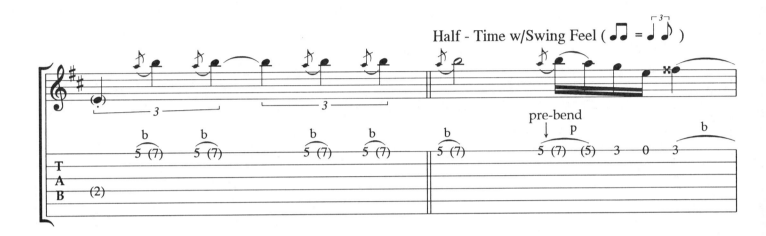

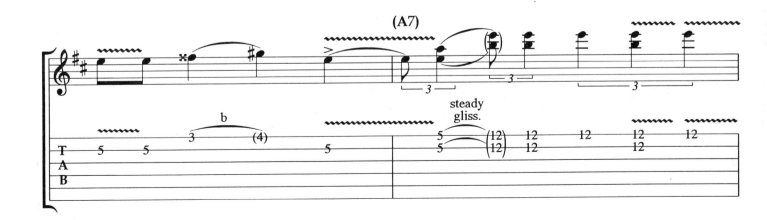

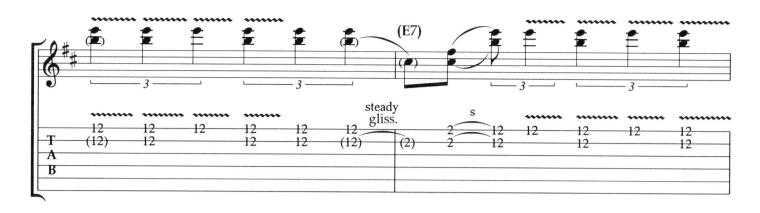

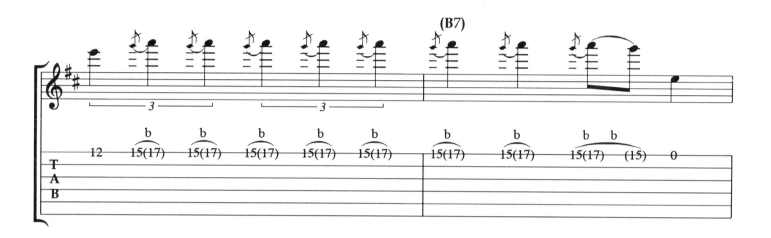

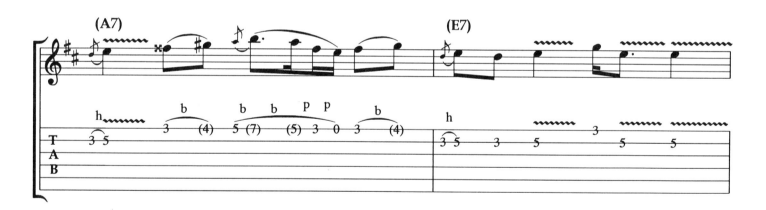

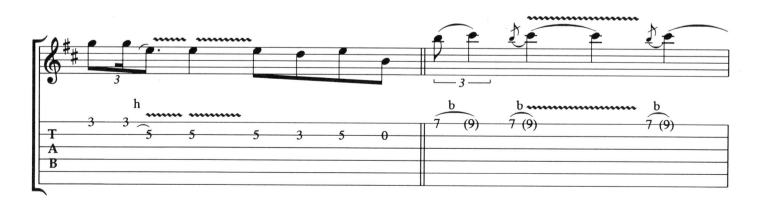

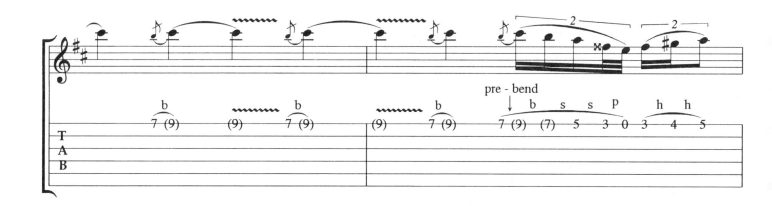

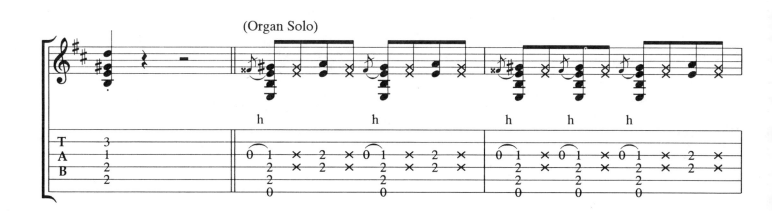

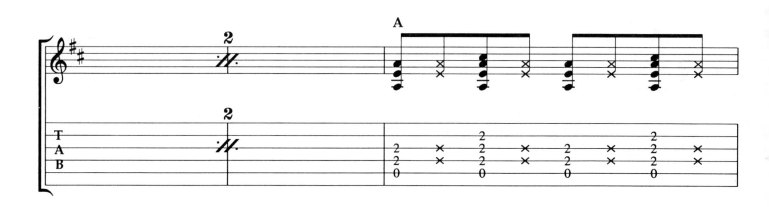

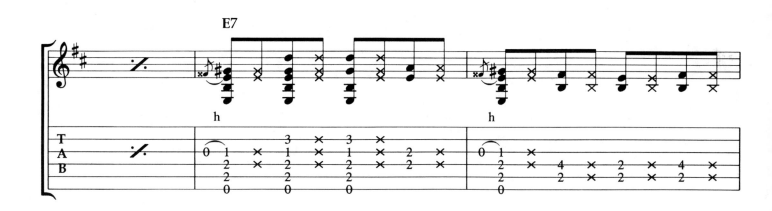

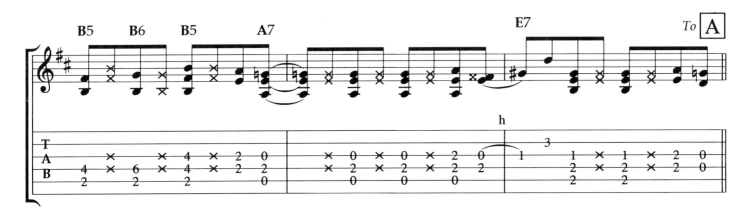

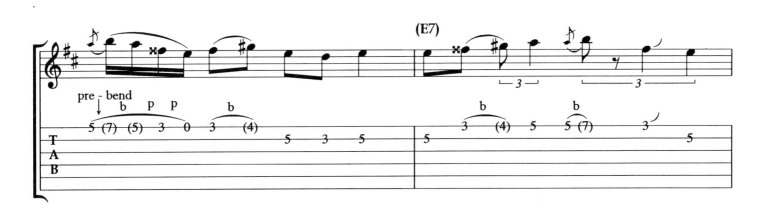

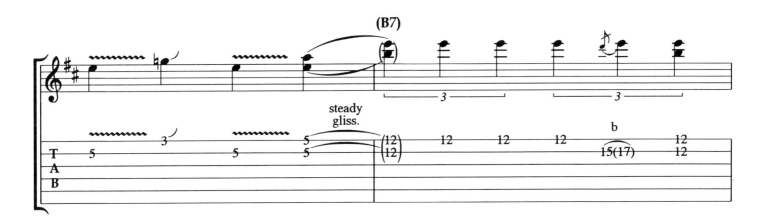

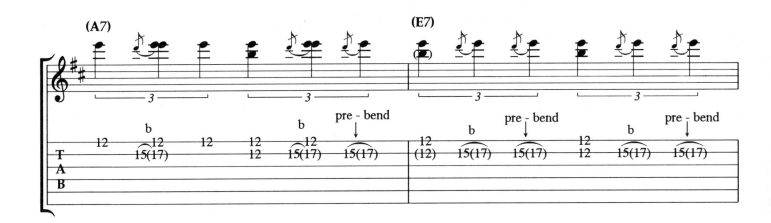

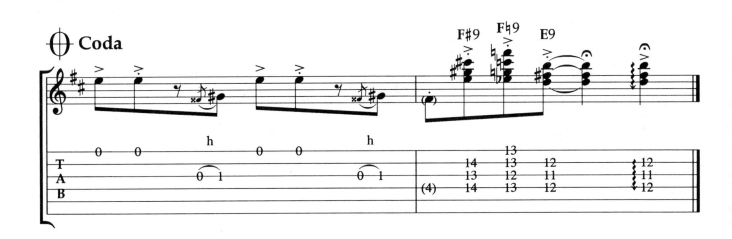

DOG ME AROUND

Transcribed Off The Recording by Howlin' Wolf on the Flair/Virgin CD "Howlin' Wolf Rides Again"

Guitar Tablature Transcription
by
Billy Simms

Words and Music by
Chester Burnett (Howlin' Wolf)
and Jules Taub

Standard Tuning:
⑥ = E ④ = D ② = B
⑤ = A ③ = G ① = E

Moderate Blues

1. How ma-ny

let ring _ _ _ _ _ _ _ _ _ _ _ _ _

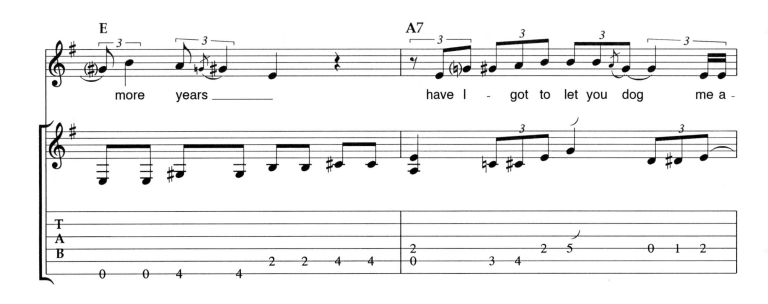

more years _____   have I - got to let you dog me a -

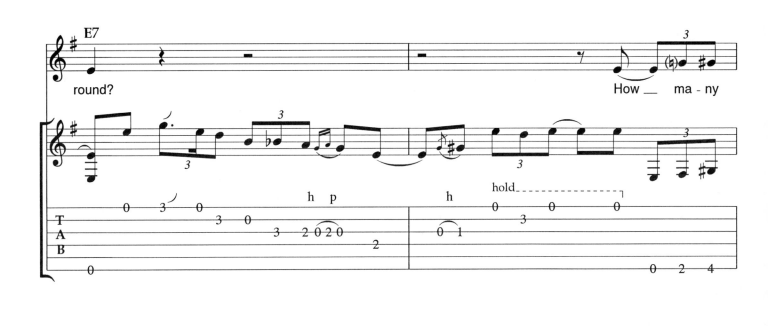

round?   How __ ma - ny

more years ___   have I ___ got to let you dog me a -

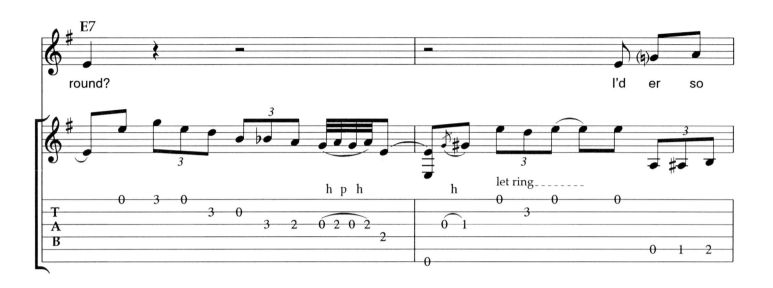

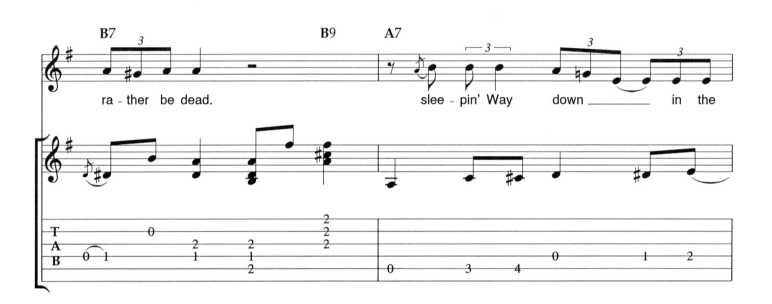

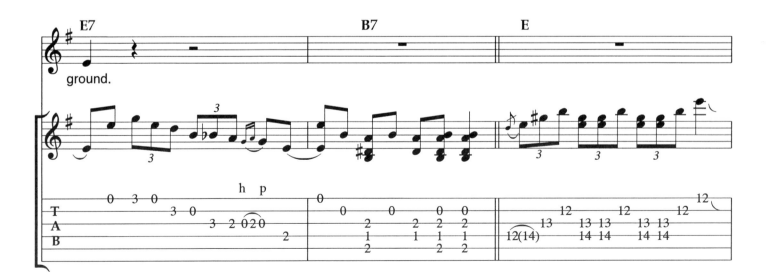

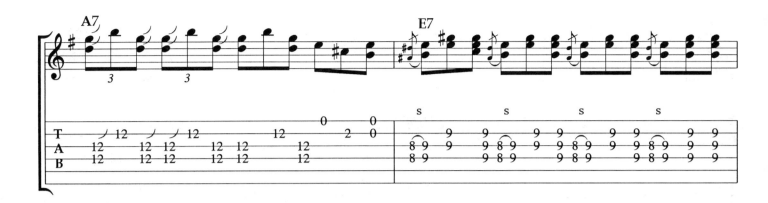

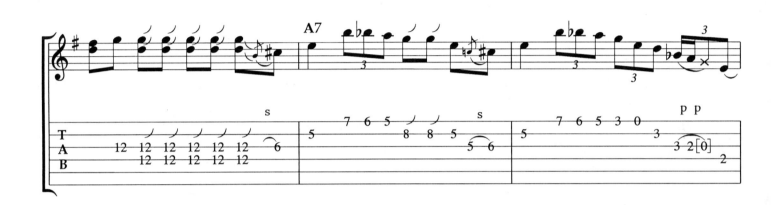

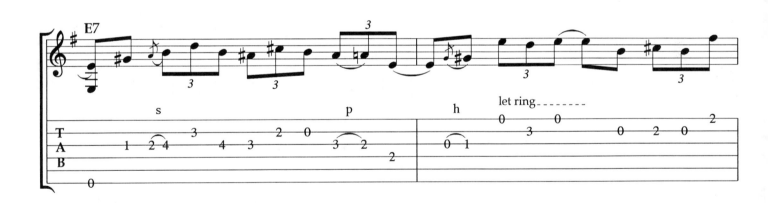

72

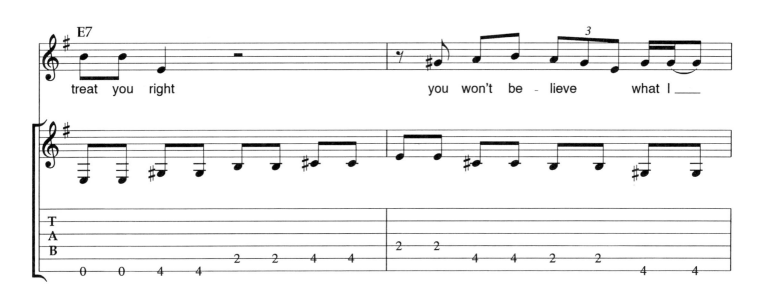

treat you right you won't be - lieve _____ What I

said you bet I'm half_

_____ way cra - zy you think I ought to let you have your way.

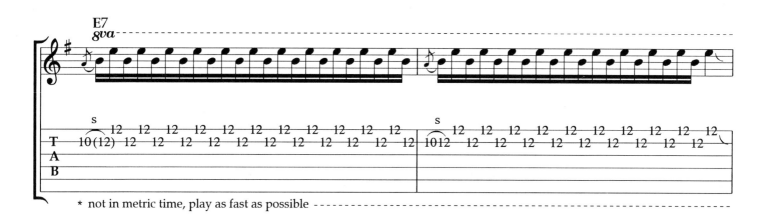

* not in metric time, play as fast as possible -

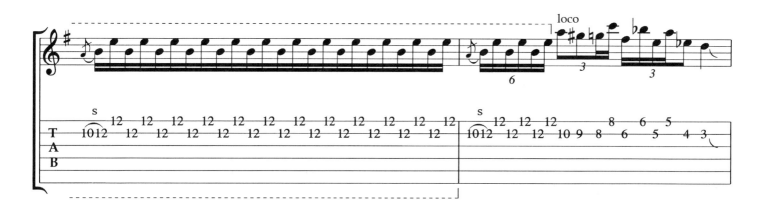

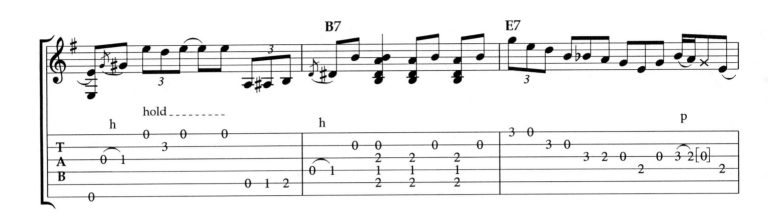

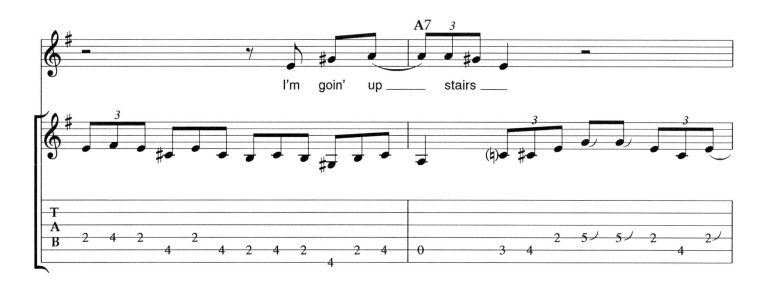

I'm goin' up ___ stairs ___

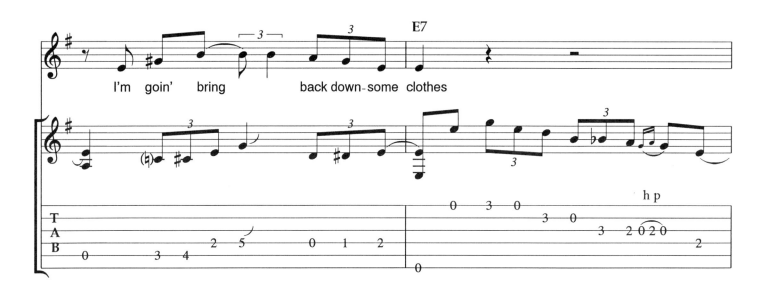

I'm goin' bring ___ back down-some clothes

If a - ny bo - dy asks a - bout me

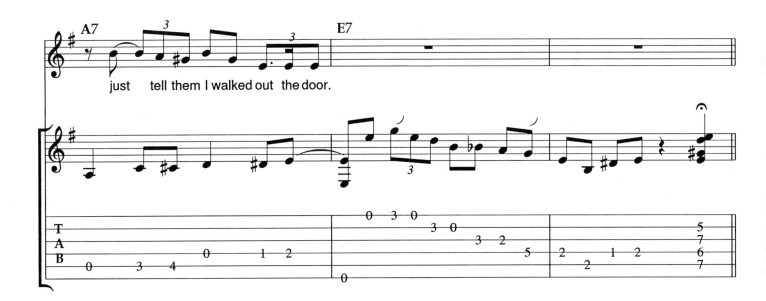

just   tell them I walked out the door.

THE FREEZE

Transcribed Off The Recording by Albert Collins on the Rhino CD entitled "The Blues Masters Vol. #3 - Texas Blues"

Guitar Tablature Transcription
by
Billy Simms

Music by
Albert Collins

F Minor Tuning:

⑥ = F   ④ = F   ② = C

⑤ = C   ③ = A♭   ① = F

Mambo

capo at 9th fret

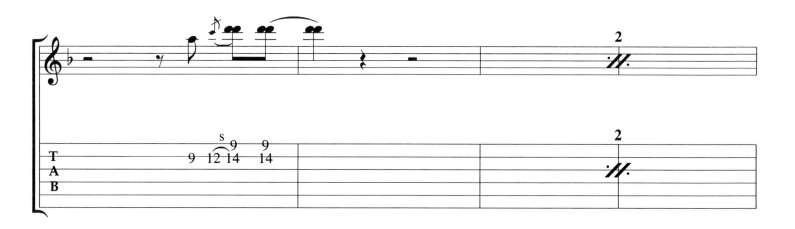

To Coda

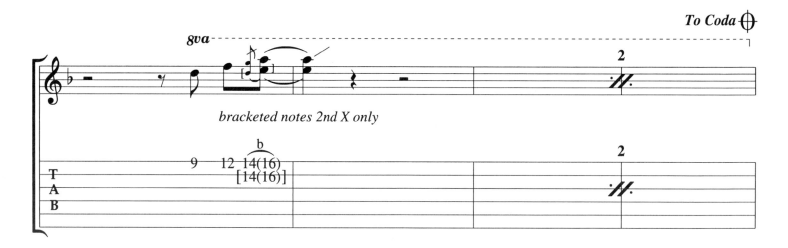

bracketed notes 2nd X only

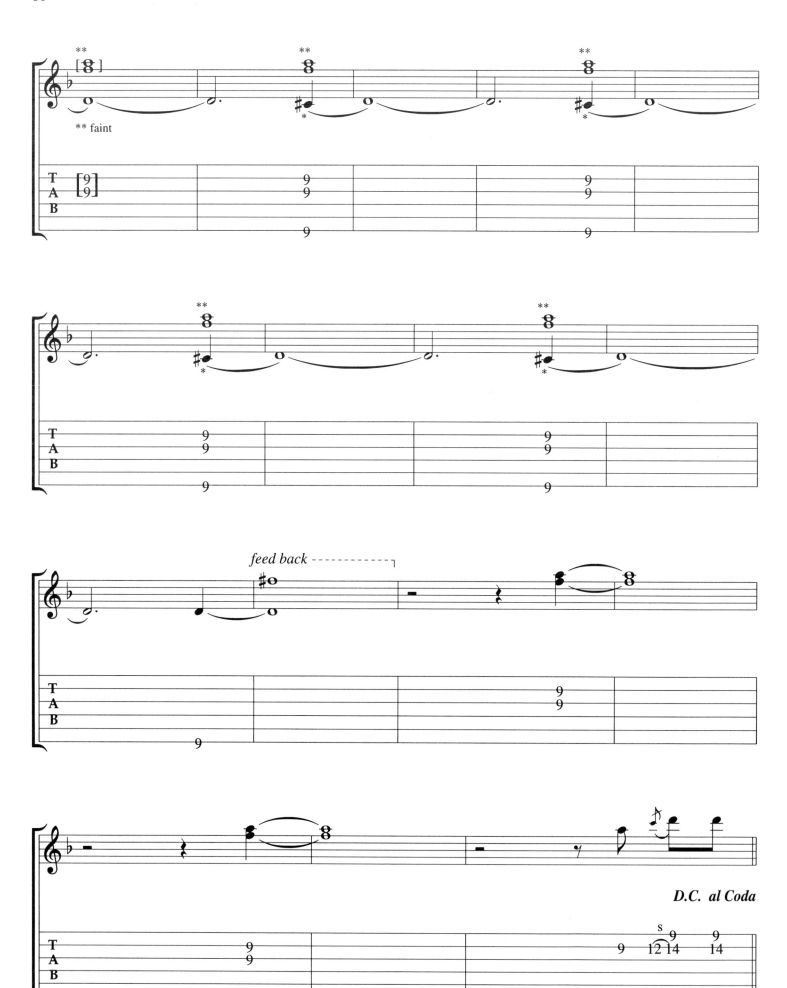

⊕ Coda

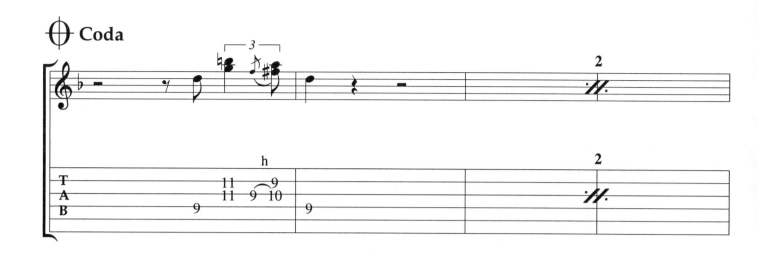

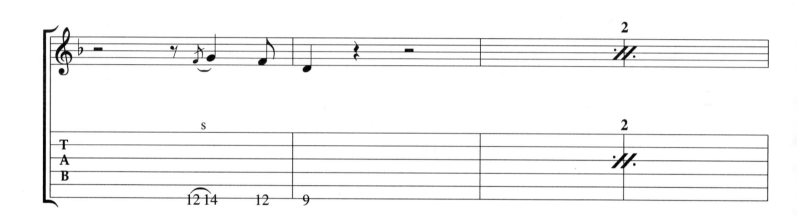

Fade Out

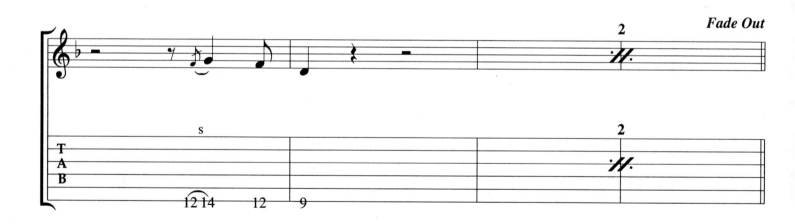

GET OUT OF HERE

Transcribed Off The Recording by B. B. King on the Flair/Virgin CD "The Best of B. B. King Vol. 2"

Guitar Tablature Transcription
by
Billy Simms

Words and Music by
Riley B. King and Sam Ling

Standard Tuning:

⑥ = E   ④ = D   ② = B
⑤ = A   ③ = G   ① = E

Medium Blues Shuffle

Triplet feel

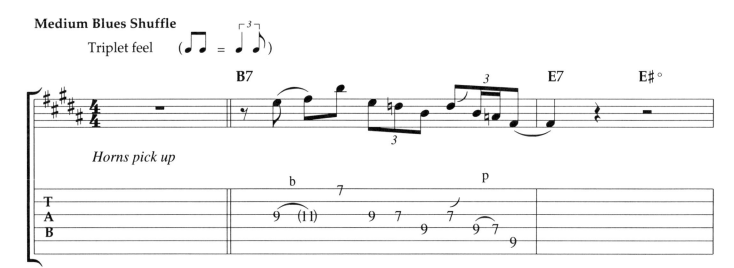

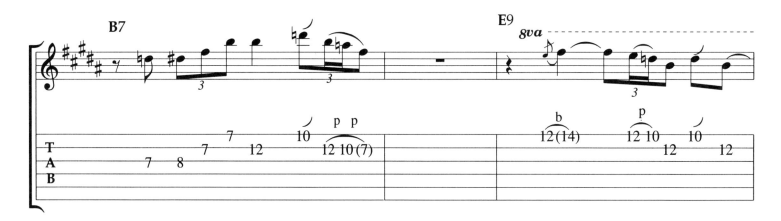

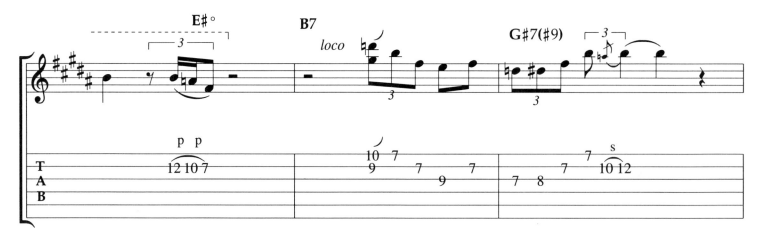

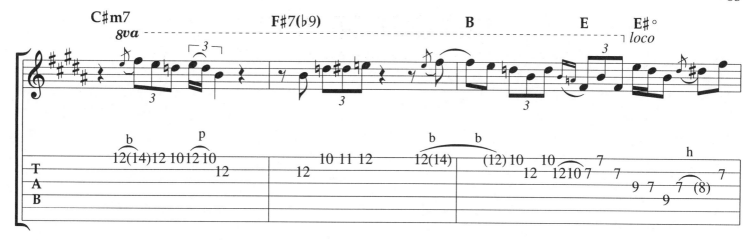

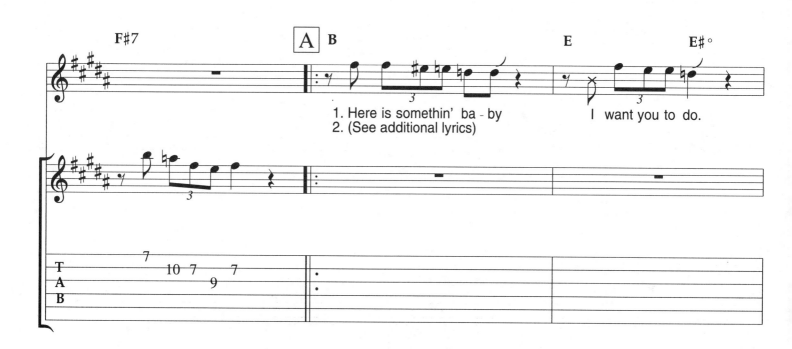

1. Here is somethin' ba - by   I want you to do.
2. (See additional lyrics)

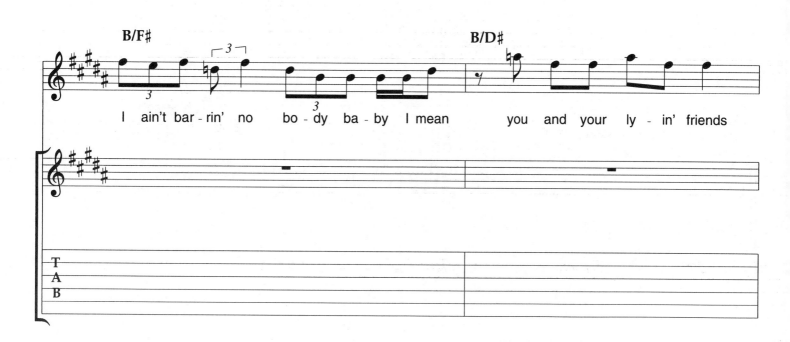

I ain't bar - rin' no bo - dy ba - by I mean   you and your ly - in' friends

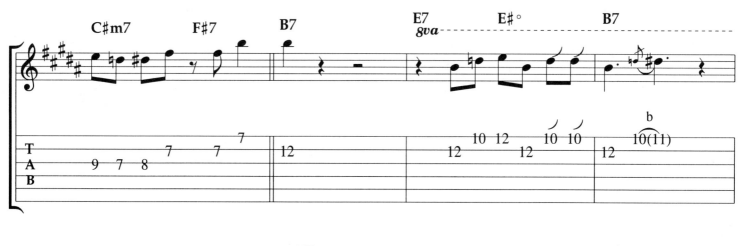

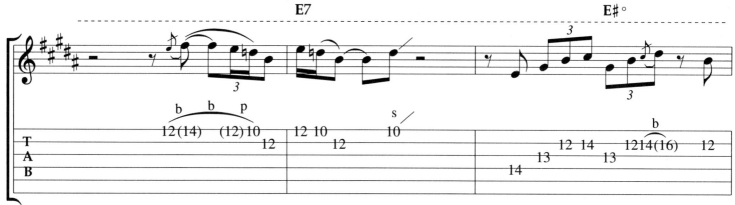

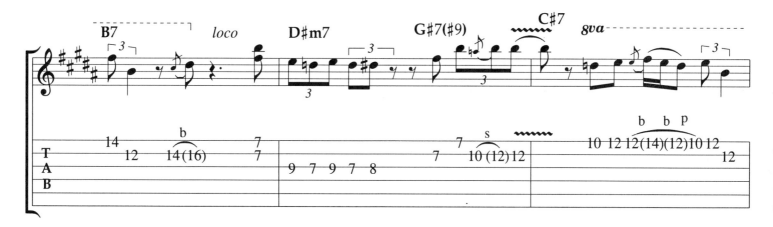

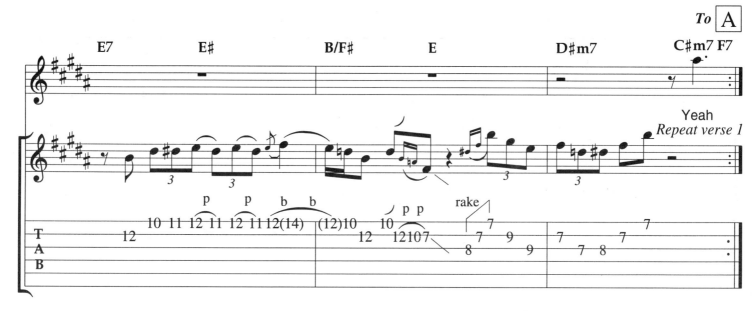

Coda

get on – out-ta here.

You and your friends –

you say you had fun

you went every place __ wo-man that you

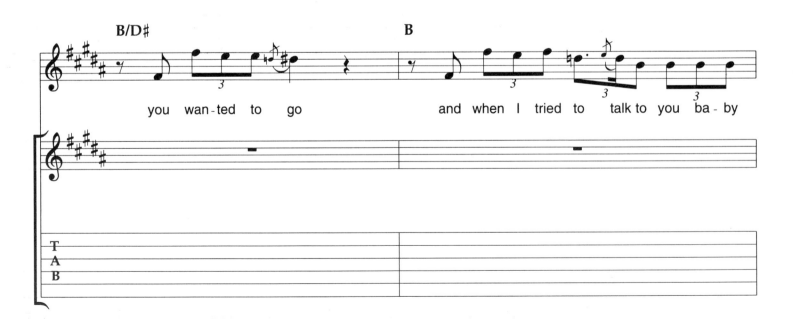

you wan-ted to go

and when I tried to talk to you ba-by

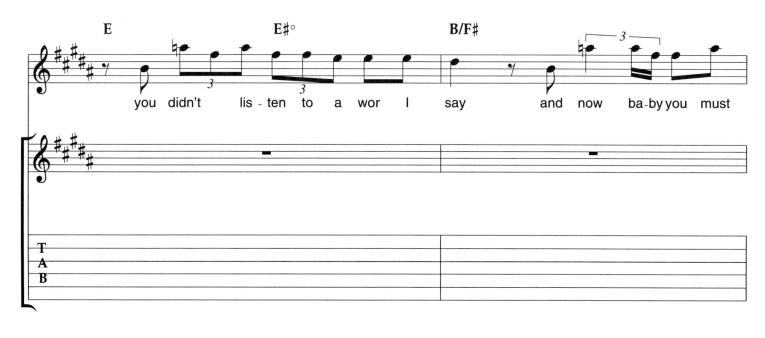

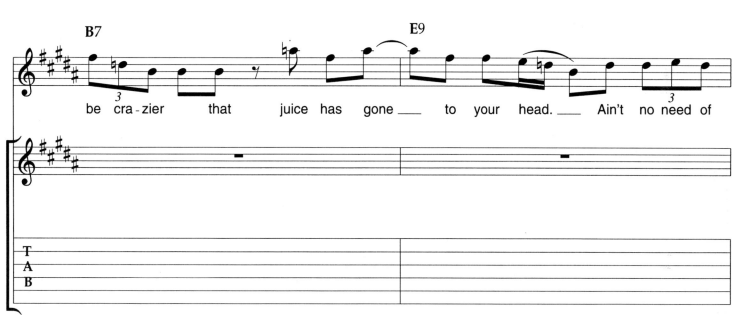

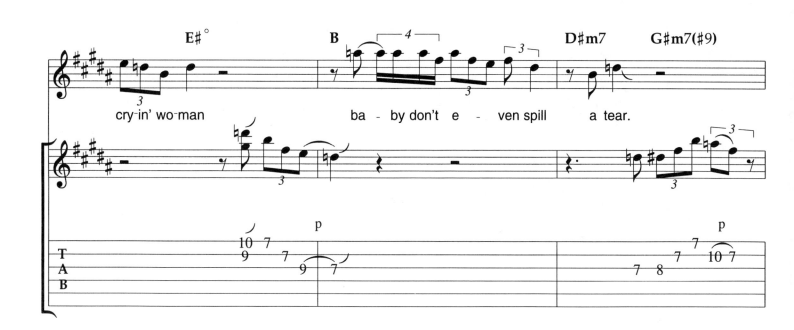

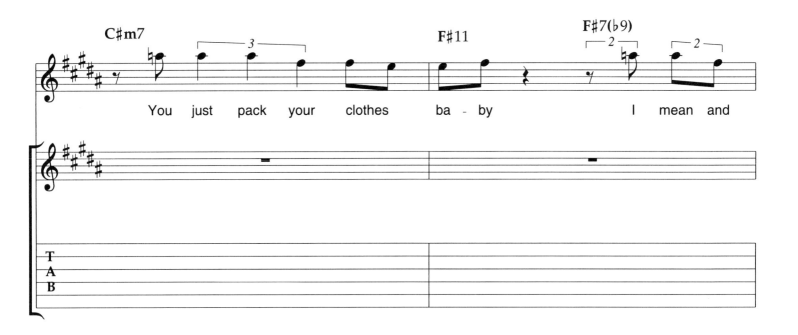

Additional Lyrics

2. I gave you a chance and that you know.
   You got greedy and thirsty baby and you spent more and more.
   There's no need cryin' baby, don't even spill a tear.
   You just pack your clothes baby, baby and get on outta here.

PRESSURE COOKER

Transcribed Off The Recording by Clarence "Gatemouth" Brown on the Alligator CD "Pressure Cooker"

Guitar Tablature Transcription
by
Skip Grasso

Music by
Clarence "Gatemouth" Brown

Standard Tuning:

⑥ = E ④ = D ② = B
⑤ = A ③ = G ① = E

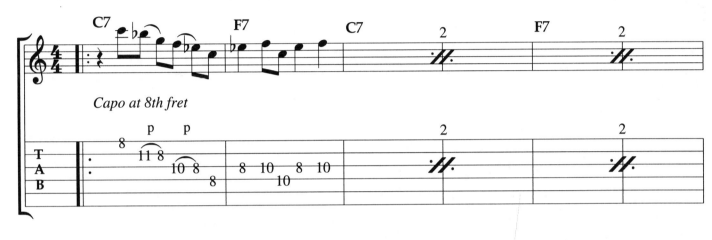

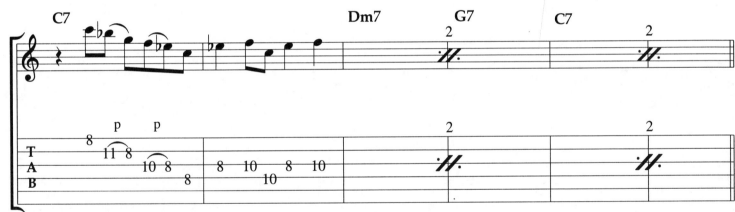

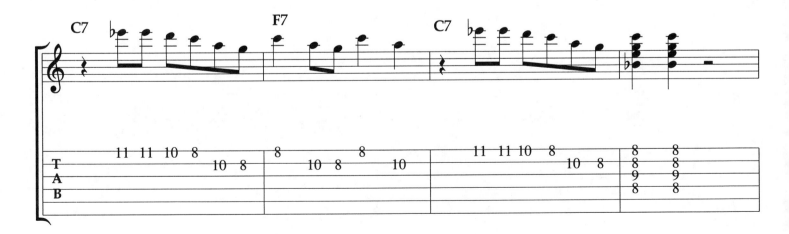

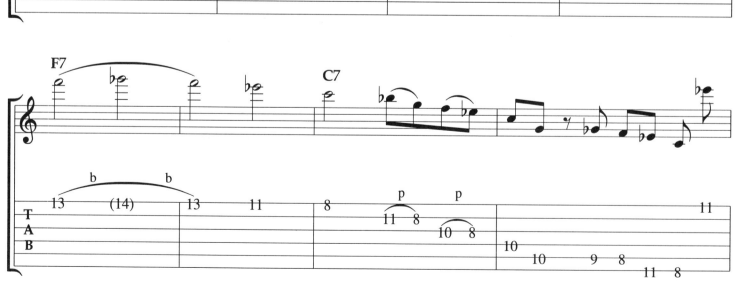

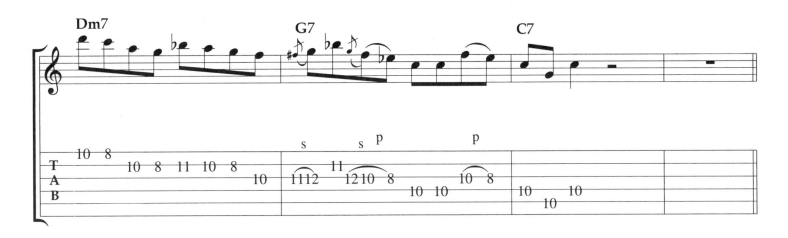

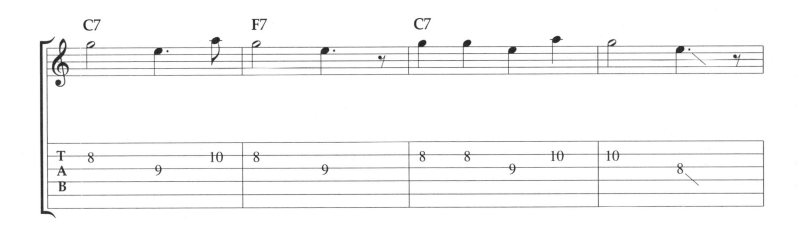

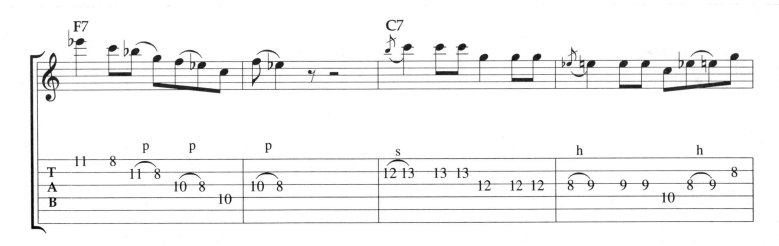

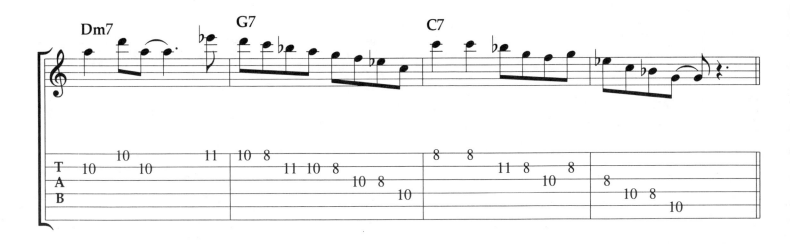

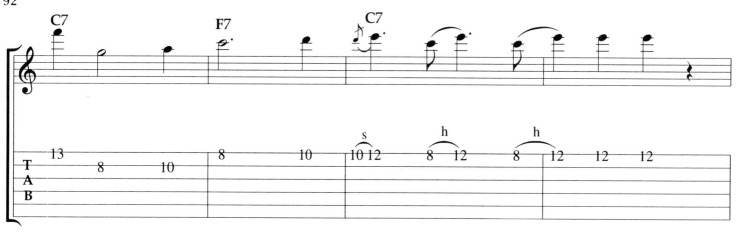

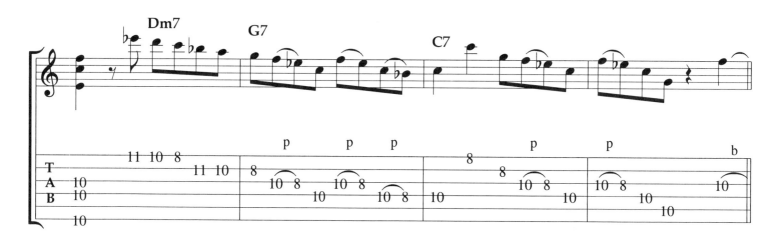

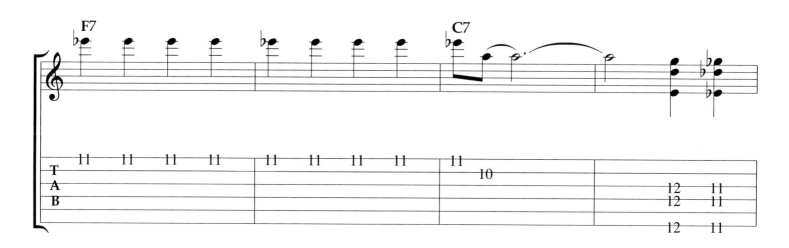

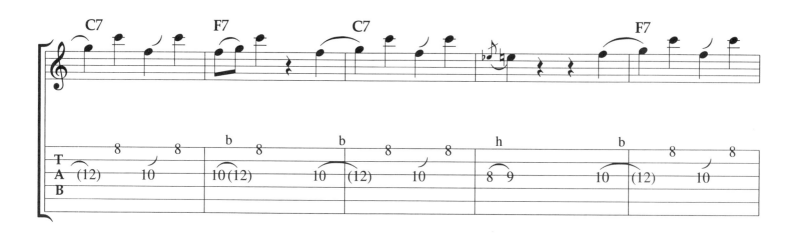

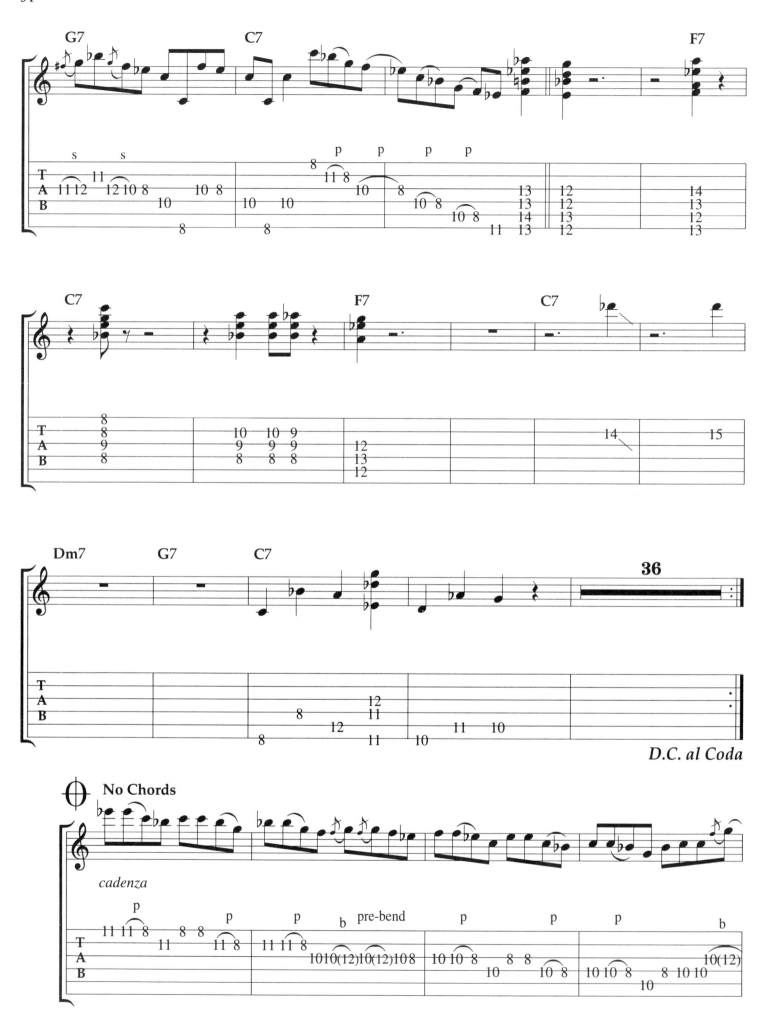

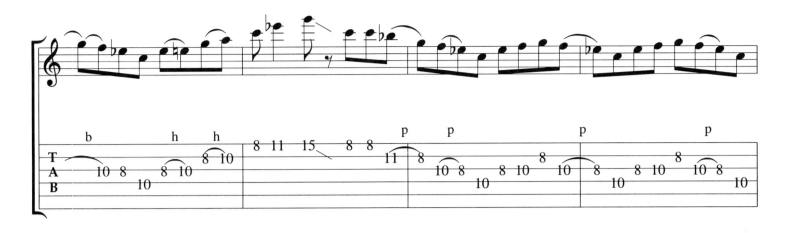

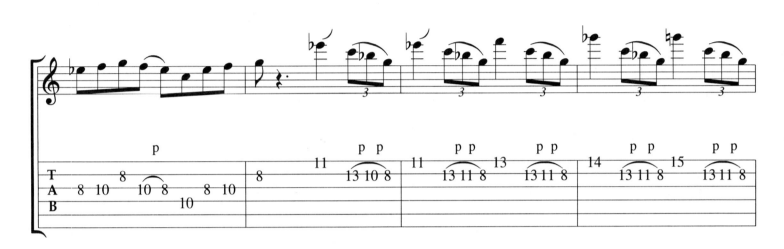

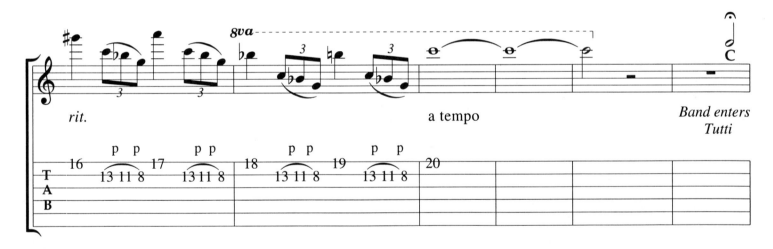

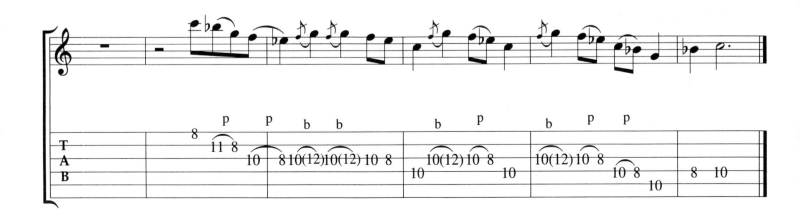

THE HUCKLE BUCK

Transcribed Off the Recording by Earl Hooker on the Rhino CD "Legends of Guitar-Electric Blues Vol. #1"

Guitar Tablature Transcription
by
Billy Simms

Words and Music by
Roy Alfred and
Andy Gibson

Standard Tuning

⑥ = E   ④ = D   ② = A
⑤ = A   ③ = G   ① = D

Fast Blues Shuffle

Triplet Feel

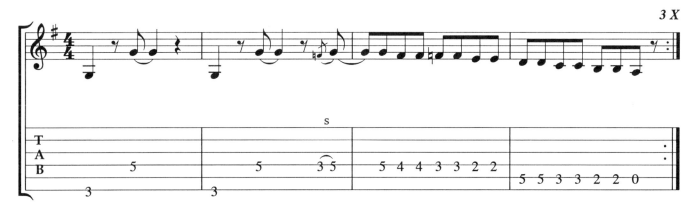

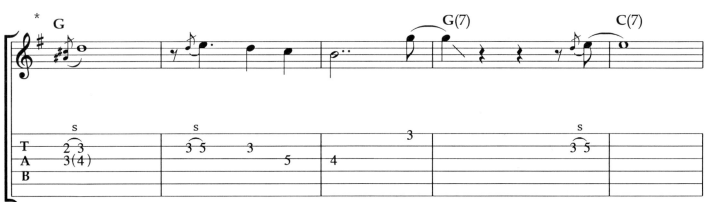

* Chord accompaniment played by piano with boogie woogie bass line.

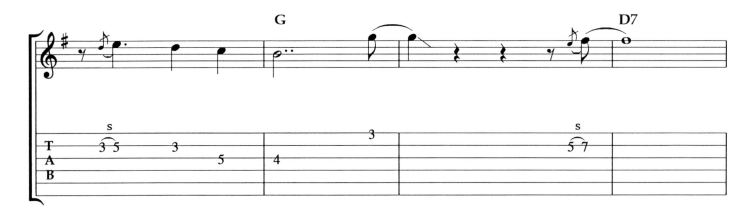

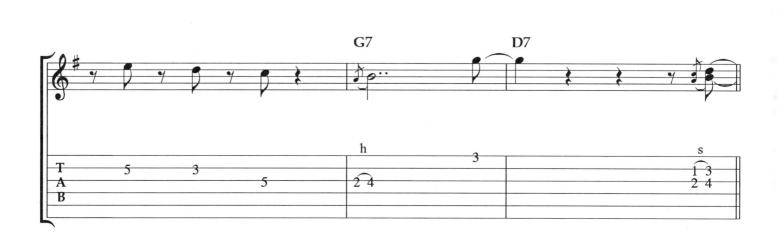

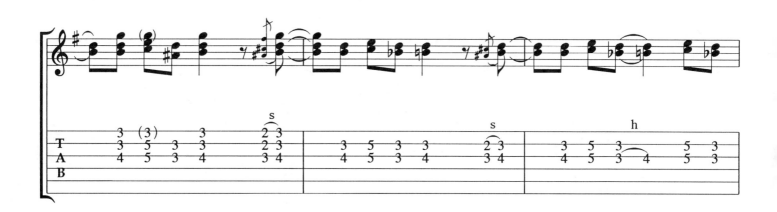

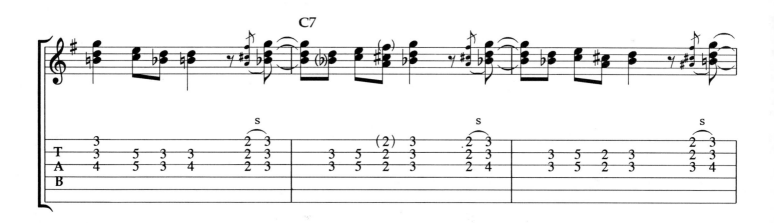

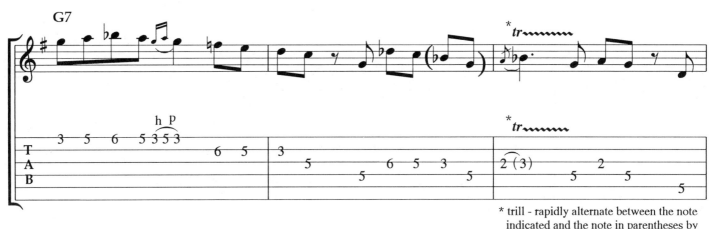

* trill - rapidly alternate between the note
indicated and the note in parentheses by
hammering on and pulling off.

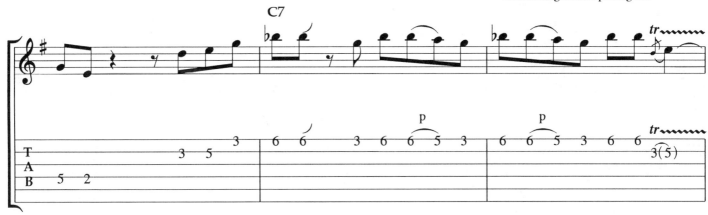

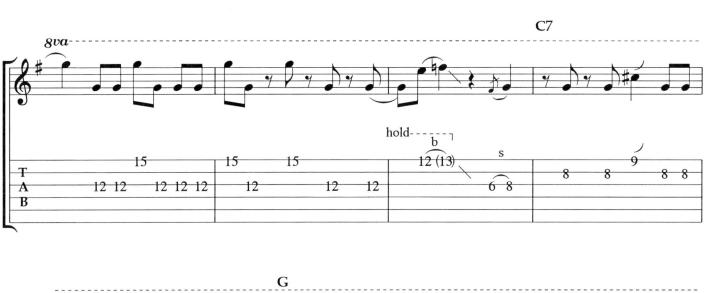

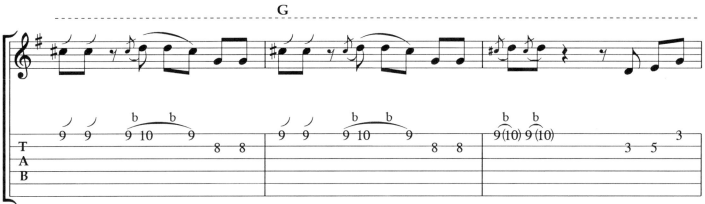

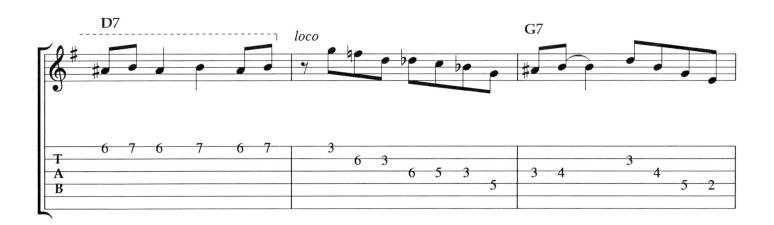

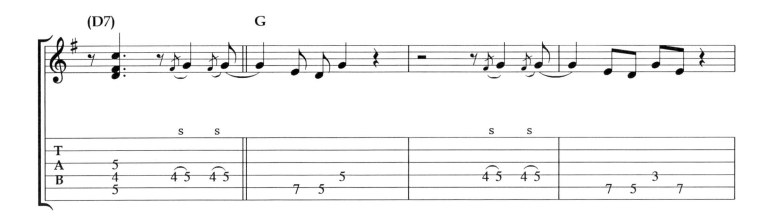

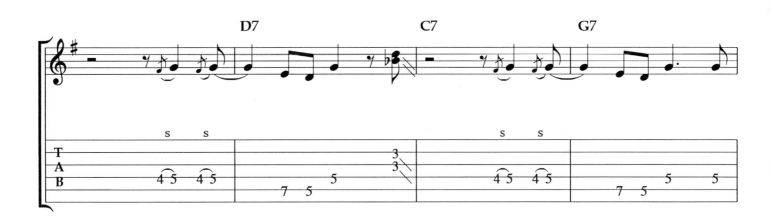

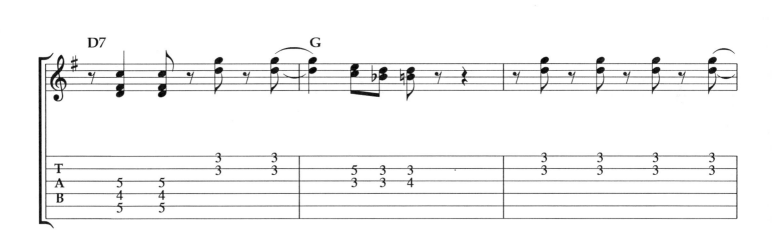

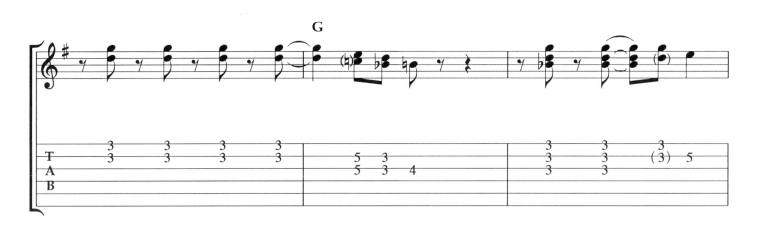

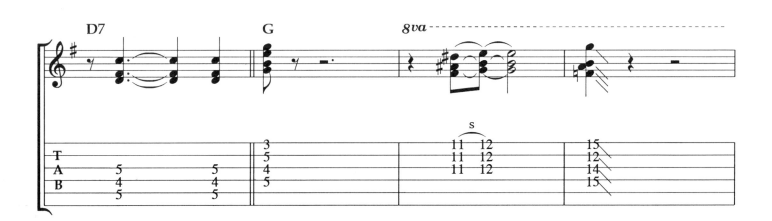

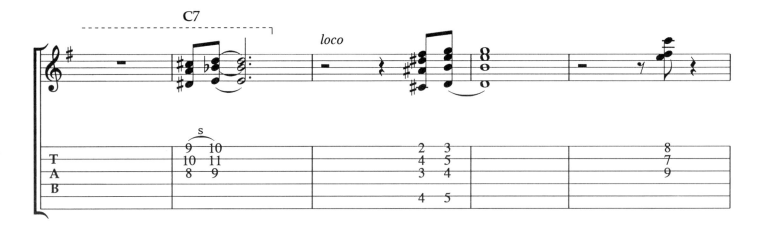

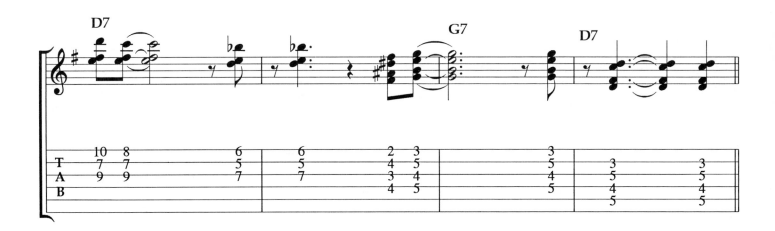

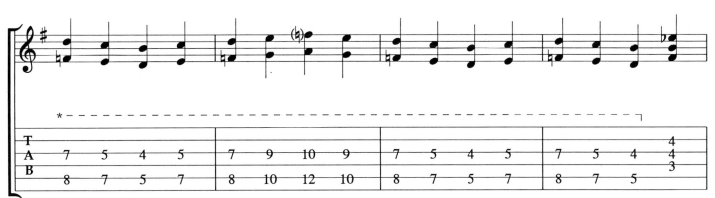

* use downstrokes - mute 4th string with whichever lefthand finger that is fretting the 5th string.

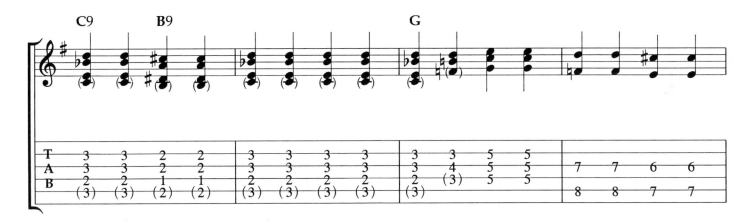

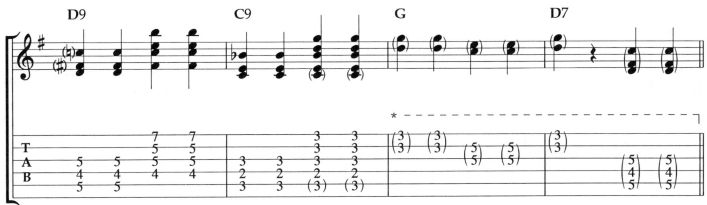

* Almost completely inaudible

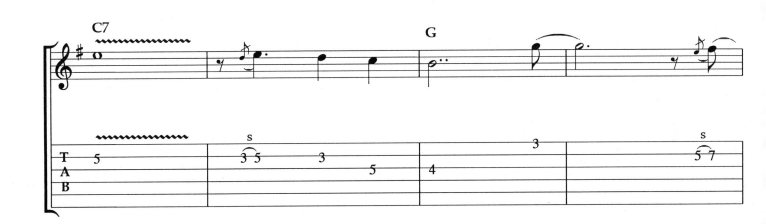

STANDING AT THE CROSSROADS

Transcribed Off The Recordings by Elmore James on The Relic Records CD "The Best of Elmore James"

Guitar Tablature Transcription
by
Billy Simms

Words and Music by
Elmore James
and Joe Josea

Open D Tuning:
⑥ = D ④ = D ② = A
⑤ = A ③ = F♯ ① = D

Moderate Blues Shuffle

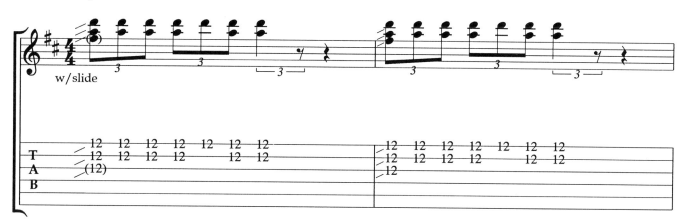

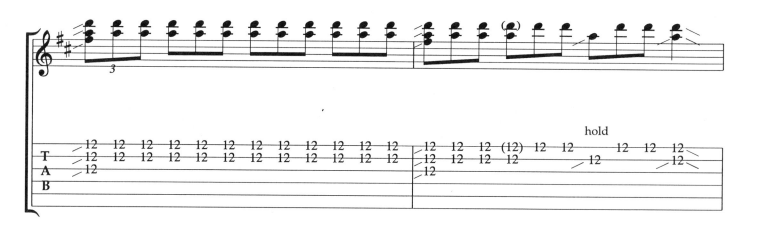

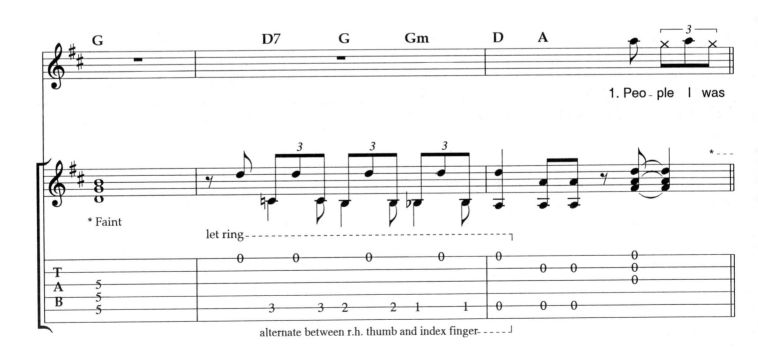

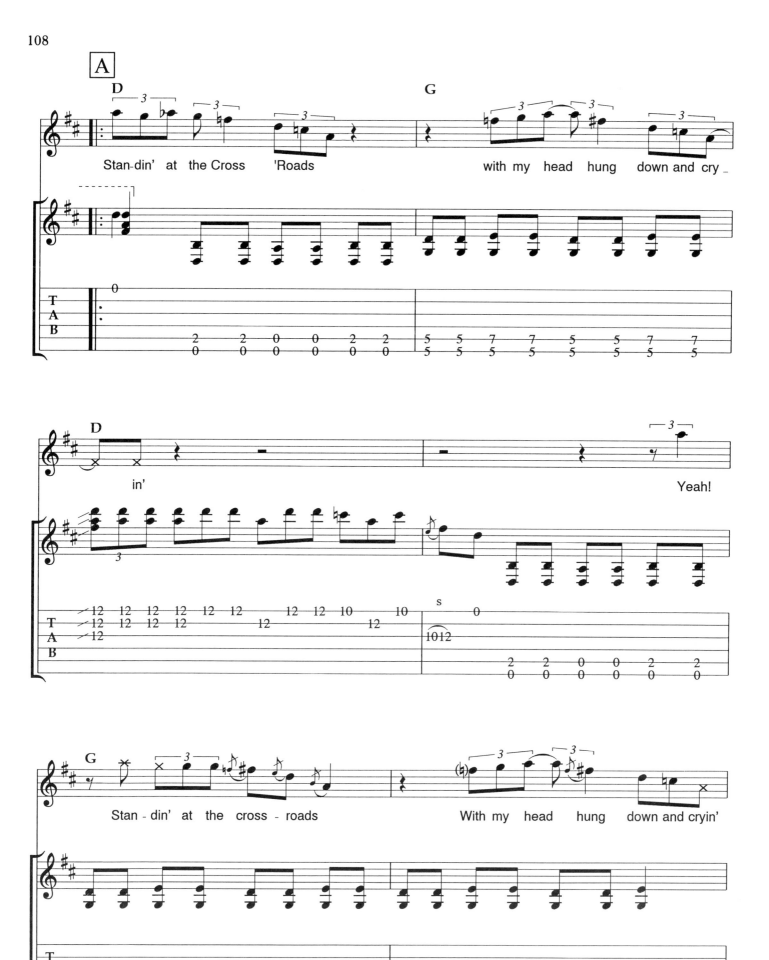

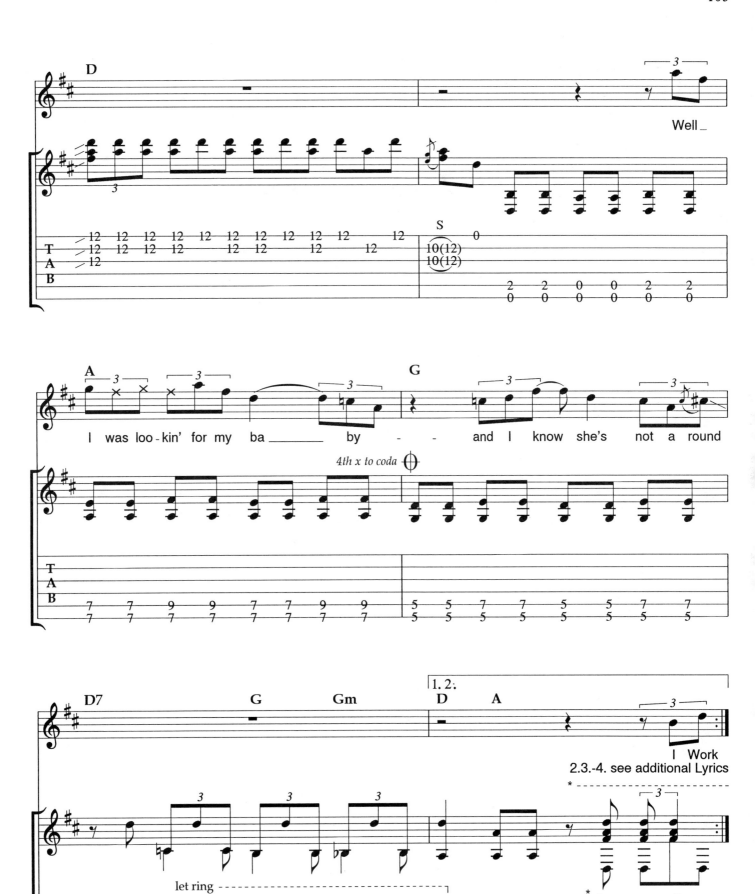

alternate between r.h. thumb and index finger - - - - - - - - - -   * upstemmed notes 2nd time only

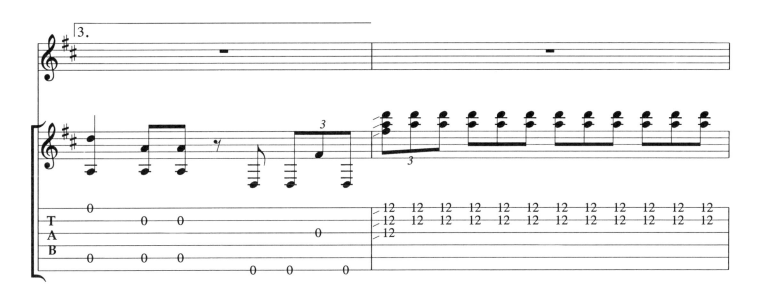

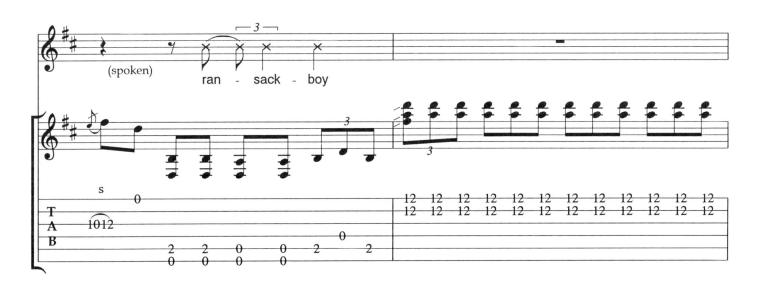

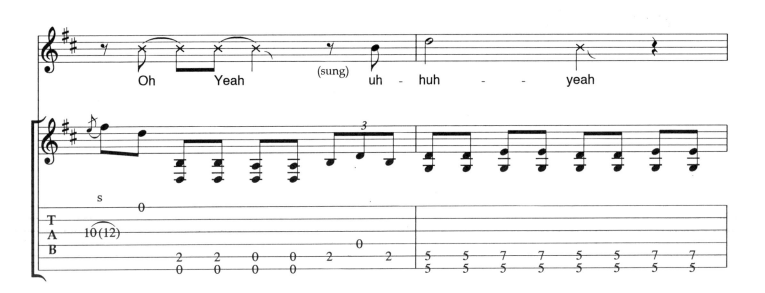

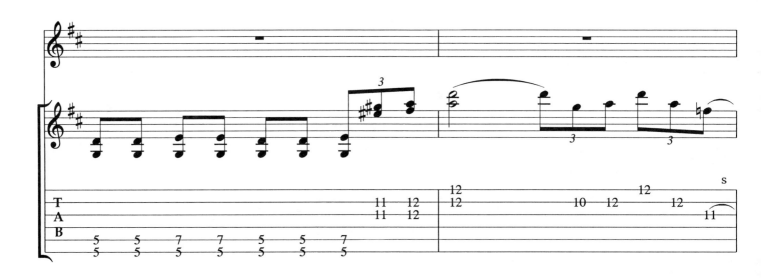

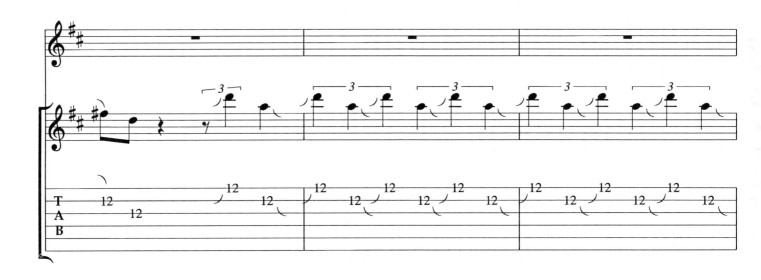

4. See additional Lyrics

Coda

She was out with another man.

Additional Lyrics

2. I work hard for my baby, she treats me like a slave.
   I work hard for my baby, She treats me like a slave.
   Well, she must be tired of livin'
   I'll put her six feet in the grave.

3. Well, I'm standing at the crossroads and my baby's not around.
   Well, I'm standing at the crossroads and my baby's not around.
   Well, I begin to wonder
   Is poor Elmore sinkin' down

4. Well, I was standing here waiting, baby, with my heart right in my hand
   Yeah, standing here waiting, baby, with my heart right in my hand
   Well, I was lookin' for my baby
   She was out with another man.

TRAMP

Transcribed Off The Recording by Lowell Fulsom on the Flair/Virgin CD "Tramp/Soul"

Guitar Tablature Transcription
by
Billy Simms

Words and Music by
Jimmy McCracklin and
Lowell Fulsom

Two Guitars: Standard Tuning

⑥ = E ④ = D ② = B
⑤ = A ③ = G ① = E

Medium Rock Groove

1. Tramp
3. See additional lyrics

Gtr. 1

Gtr. 2

You can call me that   I don't

Gtr. 1 & Gtr. 2 *

* Touch strings lightly with the fretting fingers of the left hand

after 3rd verse To Coda

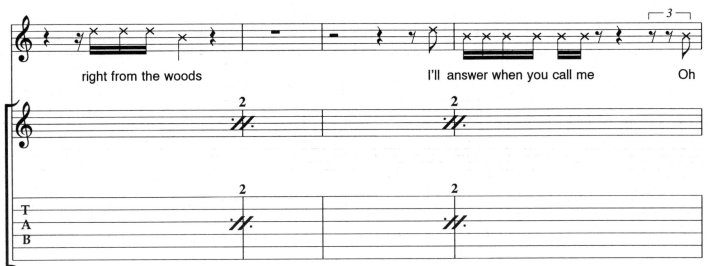

Ba-by   I mean that if it Ah_ makes you feel good   But I'm_ just a

lo - ver. _____   Ma-ma was

Pa-pa too   But I'm

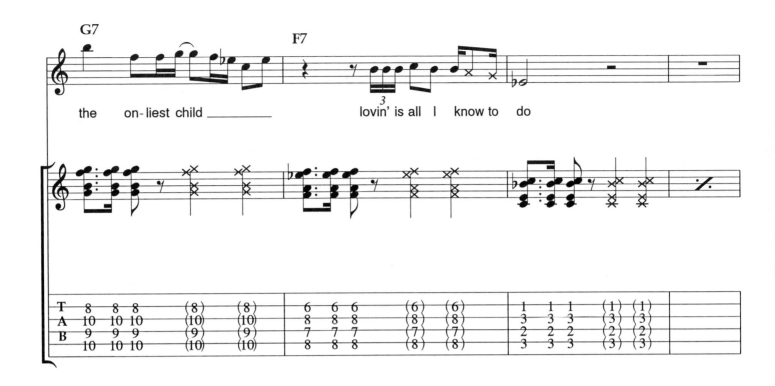

the   on-liest child _____   lovin' is all I   know to   do

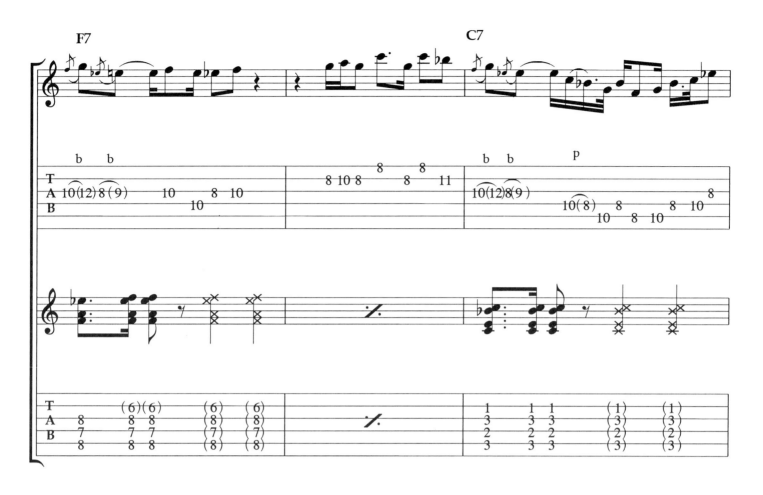

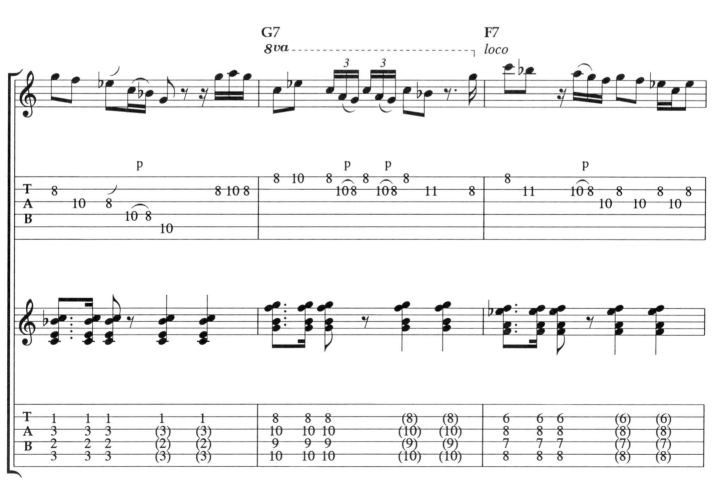

2nd Guitar (simile)

D.C. al Coda

2nd Guitar (simile)

Fade Out

* Pick down strokes as if strumming w/slight delay between notes.

2nd Guitar (simile)

Additional Lyrics

(Spoken)
Now whatever you call me
I'll even go for that
'Cause I keep a fat bank roll in my pocket
You know I own three Cadillacs

(Sing)
'Cause I'm just a lover (etc.)

WORRIED ABOUT MY BABY

Transcribed Off The Recording by Howlin' Wolf on the Flair/Virgin CD "Howlin' Wolf Rides Again"

Guitar Tablature Transcription
by
Billy Simms

Words and Music by
Chester Burnett (Howlin' Wolf)
and Jules Taub

Standard Tuning:

⑥ = E ④ = D ② = B
⑤ = A ③ = G ① = E

Fast Blues
Triplet Feel

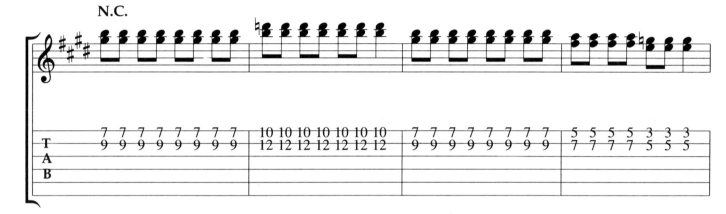

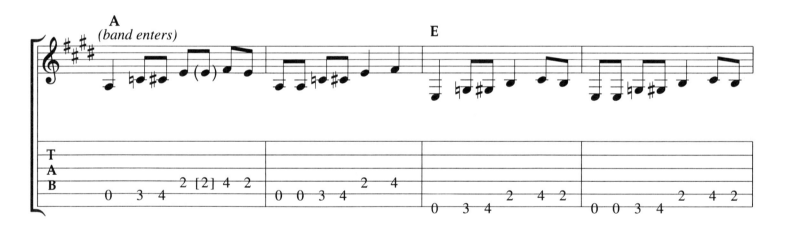

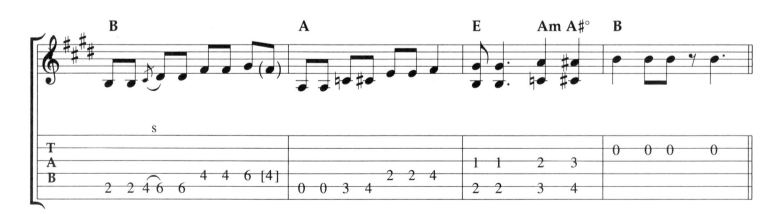

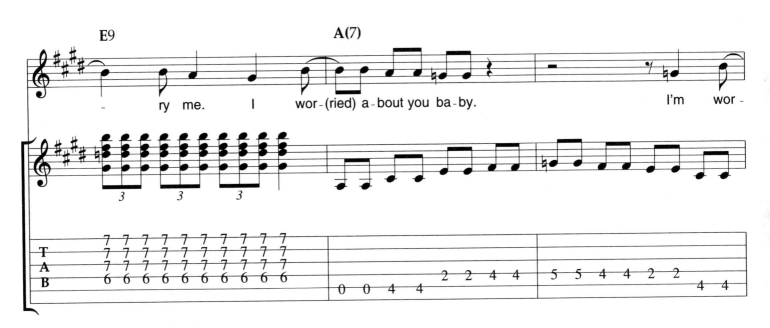

hard - ly sleep at night. ___

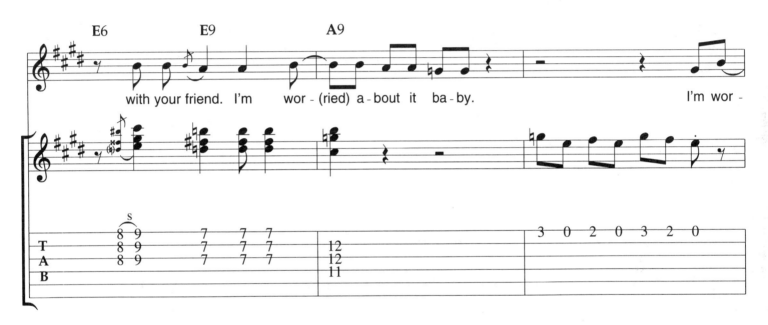

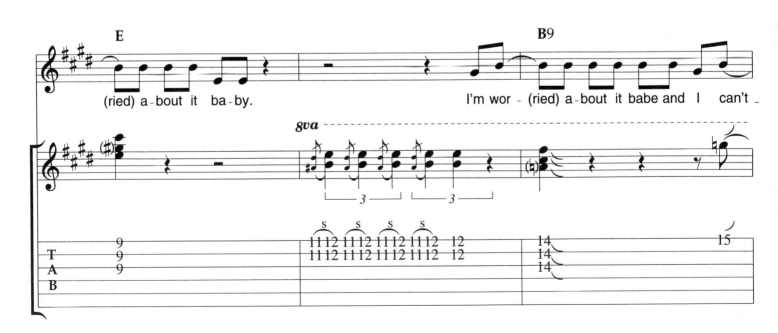

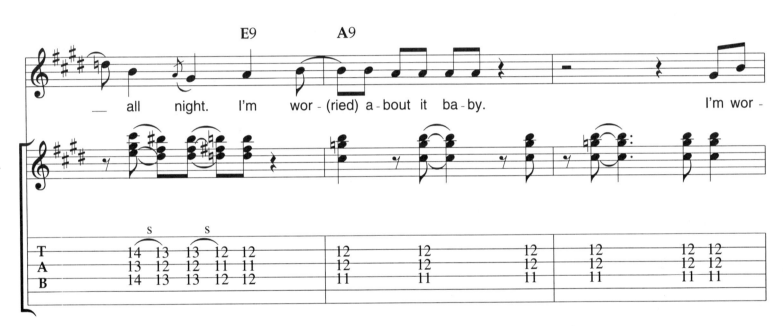

126

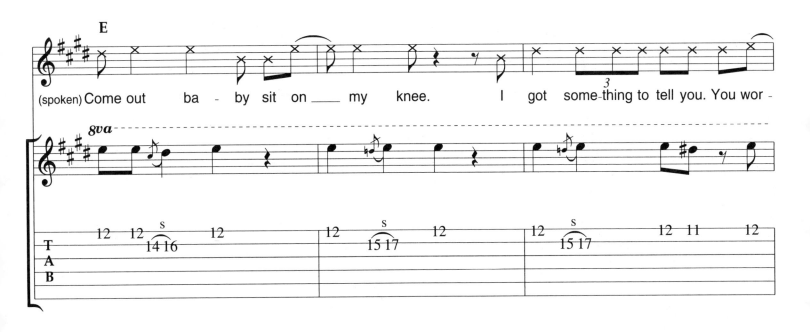

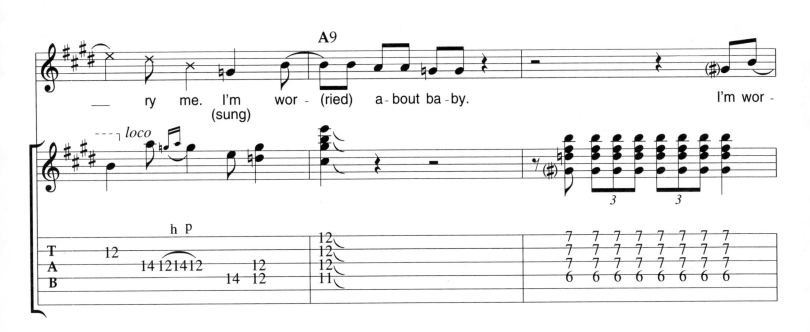

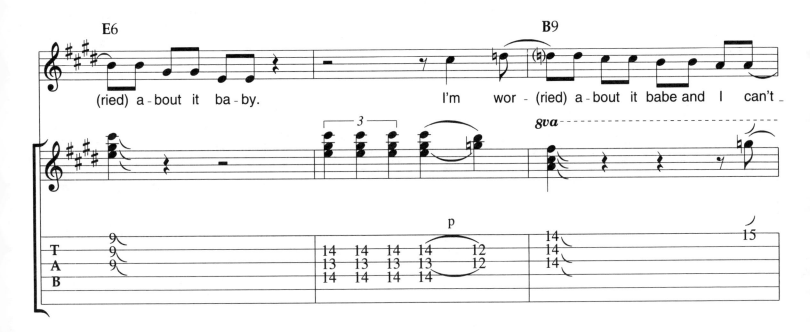

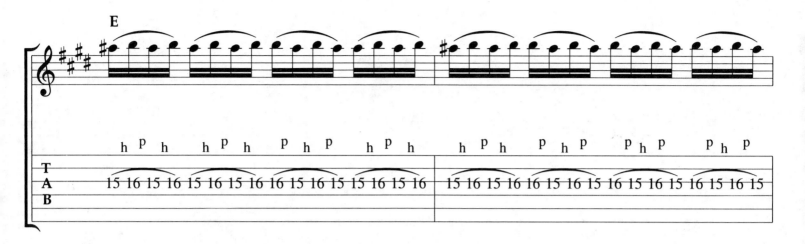

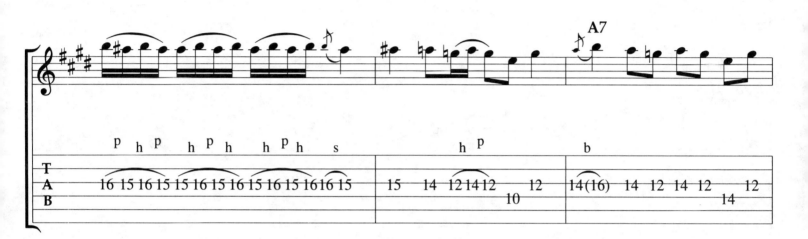

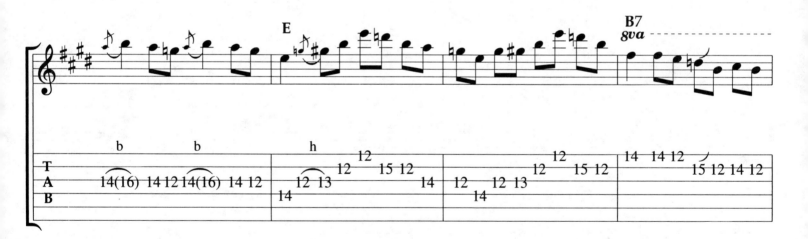

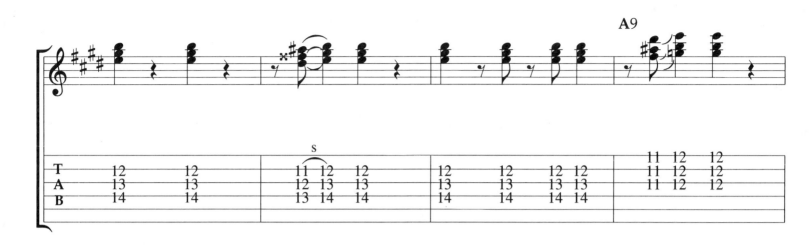

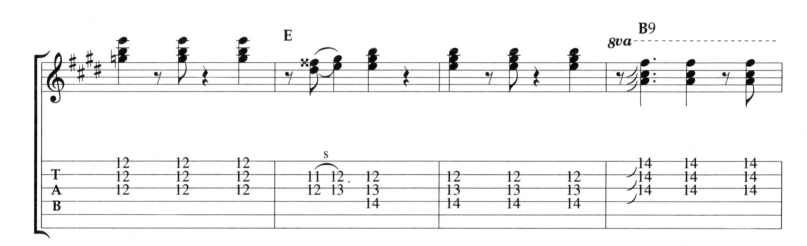

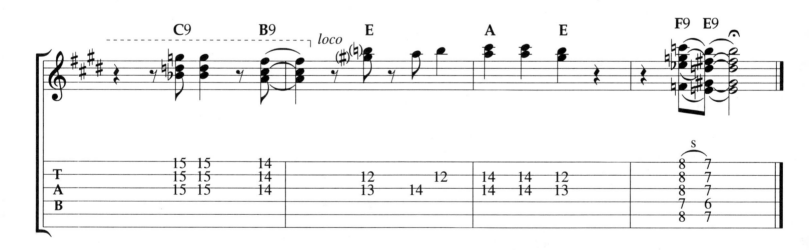

WORK SONG

Transcribed Off The Recording by THE VENTURES

Guitar Tablature Transcription
by
Roy Zimmerman

Words by Oscar Brown, Jr.
Music by Nat Adderley

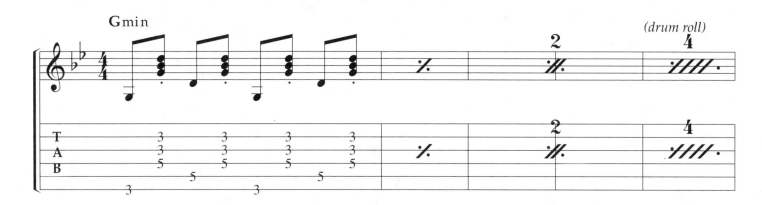

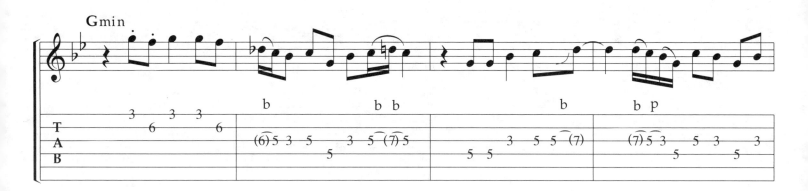

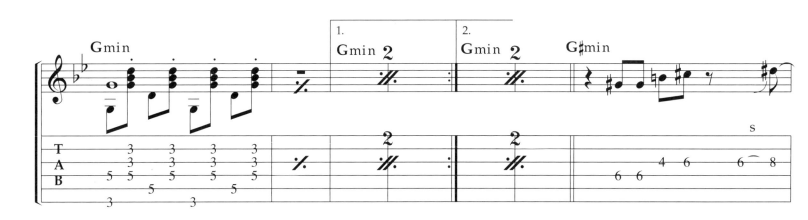

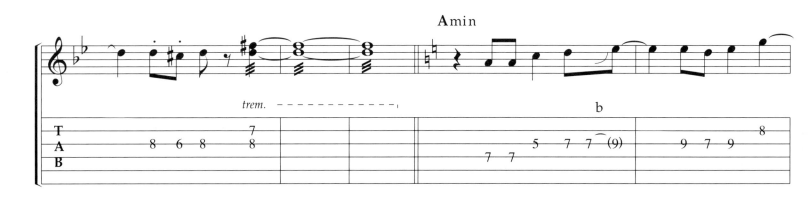

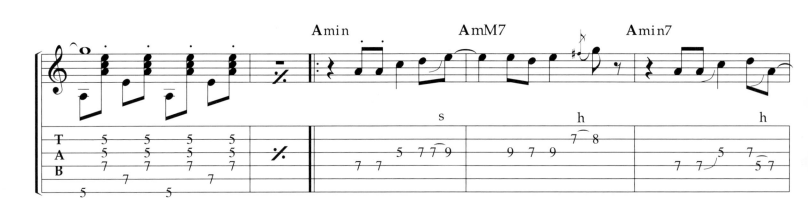

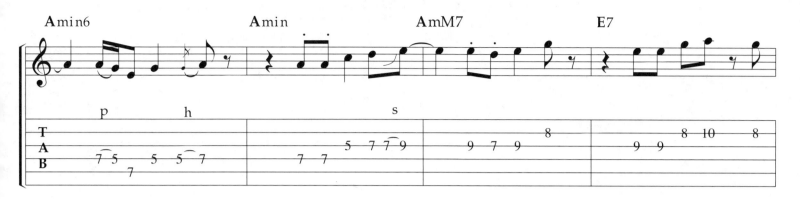

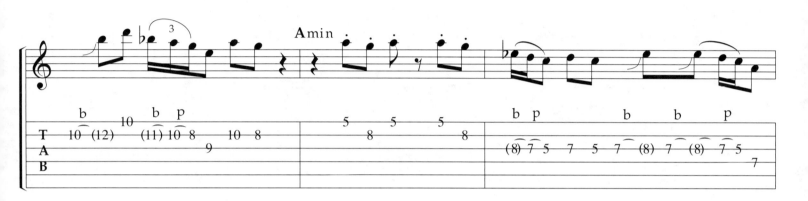

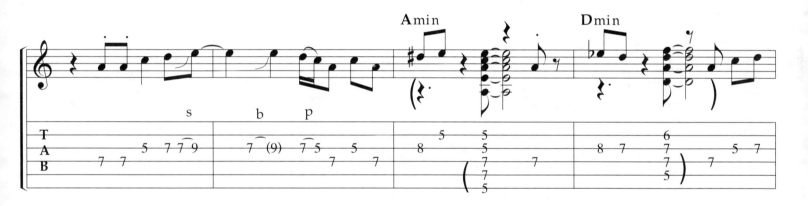

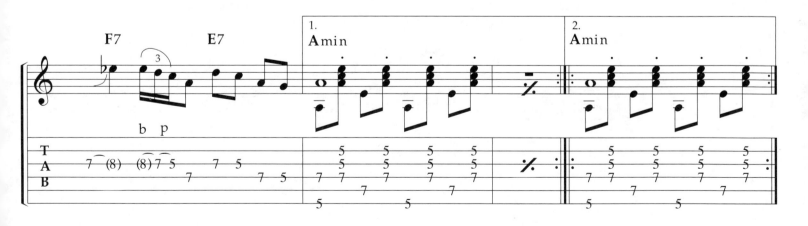

TALKIN' WOMAN

Transcribed Off The Recording by Lowell Fulsom on the Flair/Virgin CD "Lowell Fulsom : Tramp/Soul"

Guitar Tablature Transcription
by
Billy Simms
Two Guitars: Standard Tuning

⑥ = E ④ = D ② = B
⑤ = A ③ = G ① = E

Words and Music by
Lowell Fulsom
and Ferdinand "Fats" Washington

Medium Blues Shuffle

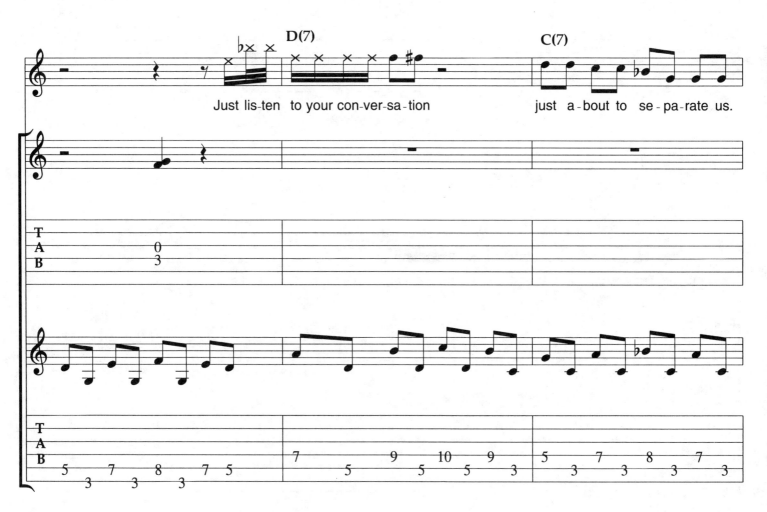

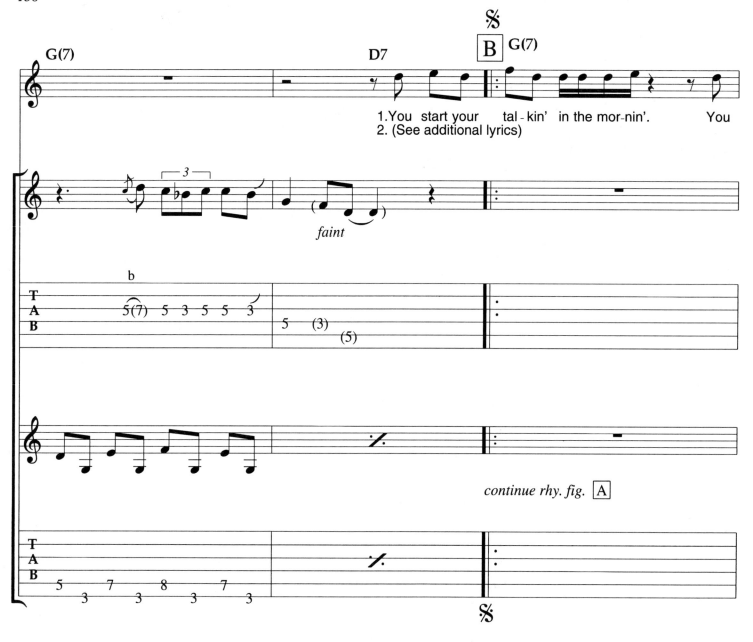

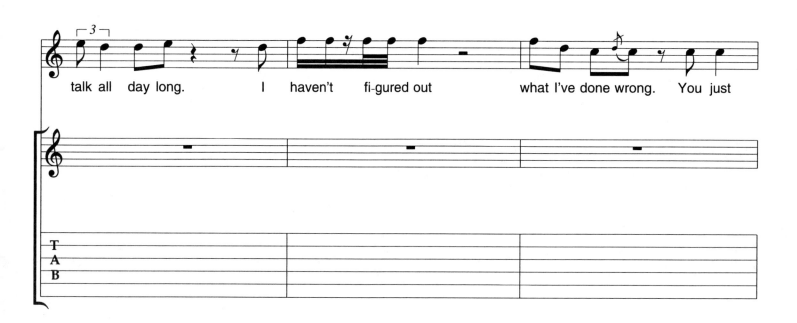

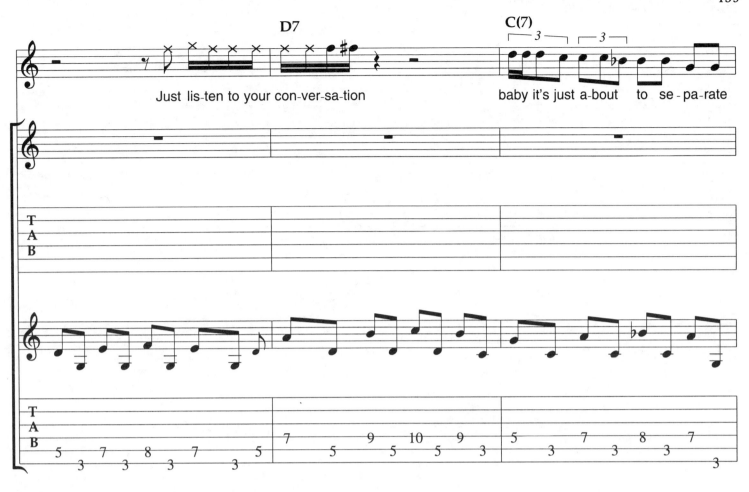

Just lis-ten to your con-ver-sa-tion

baby it's just a-bout to se-pa-rate

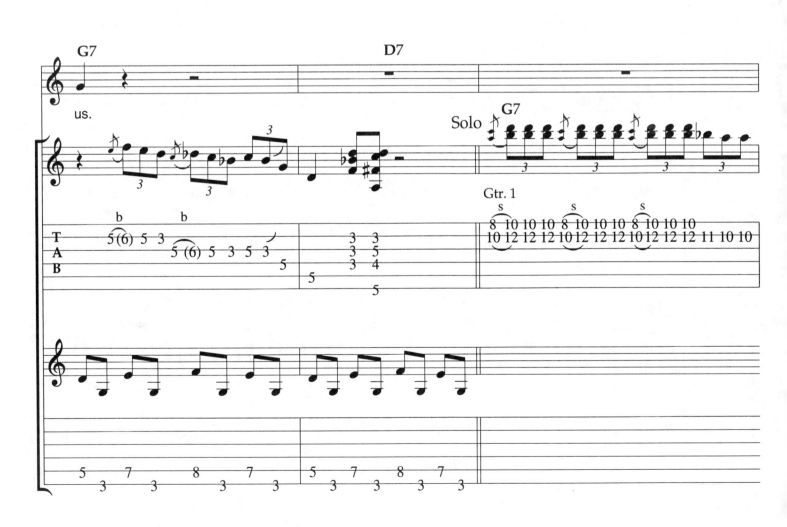

us.

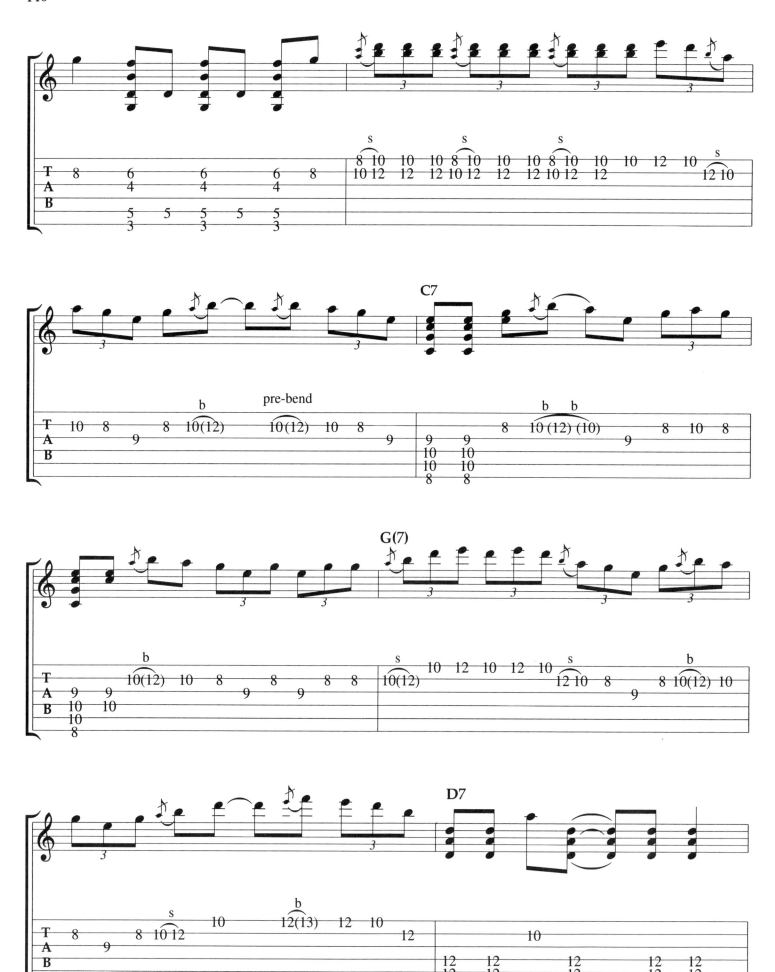

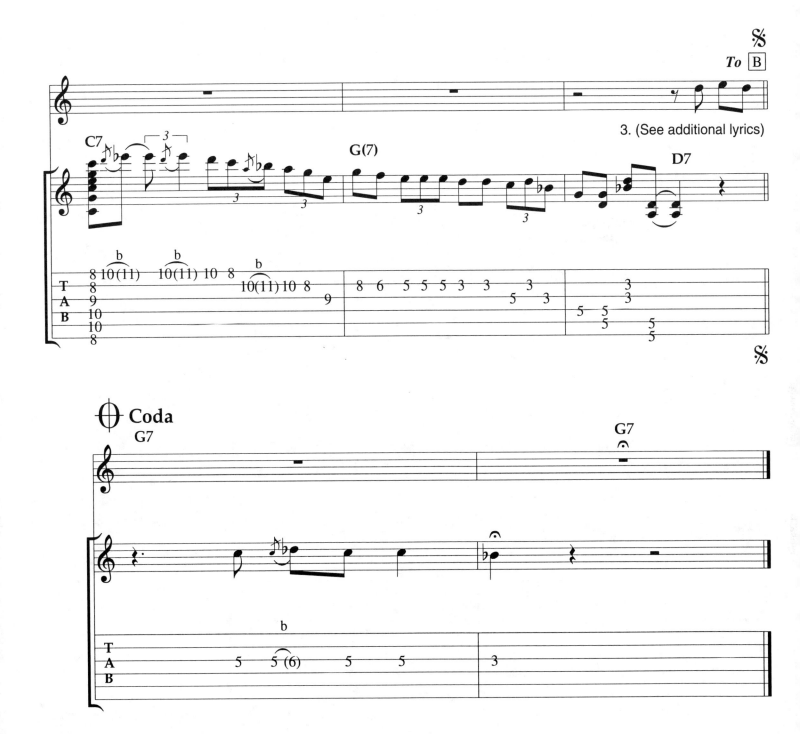

3. (See additional lyrics)

Additional Lyrics

2. I stay out late because I hate to come home.
   Everything I do baby seem to be wrong.
   You just talk so much. Yes you just talk so much.
   Just listen to your conversation just about to separate us.

3. I cook my breakfast, lunch and dinner. I do it all the time.
   You know this woman is 'bout to drive me outta my mind.
   Because she talks so much. etc.

THREE HOURS PAST MIDNIGHT

Transcribed Off The Recording by Johnny "Guitar" Watson on the Flair/Virgin CD "Three Hours Past Midnight"

Guitar Tablature Transcription
by
Billy Simms

Words and Music by
Johnny "Guitar" Watson
and Sam Ling

Standard Tuning:

⑥ = E ④ = D ② = B
⑤ = A ③ = G ① = E

Slow Blues

capo at 4th fret   * parentheses indicate incidental ringing of strings

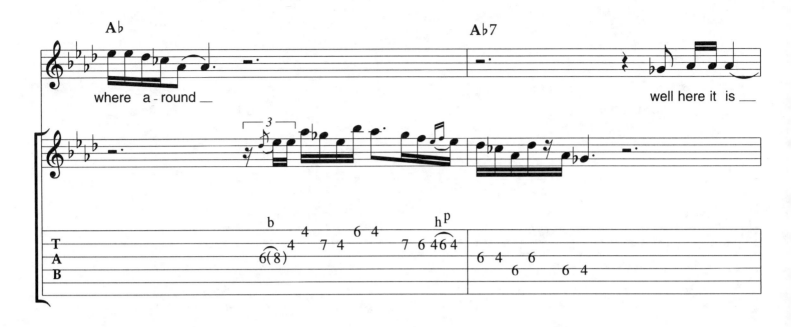

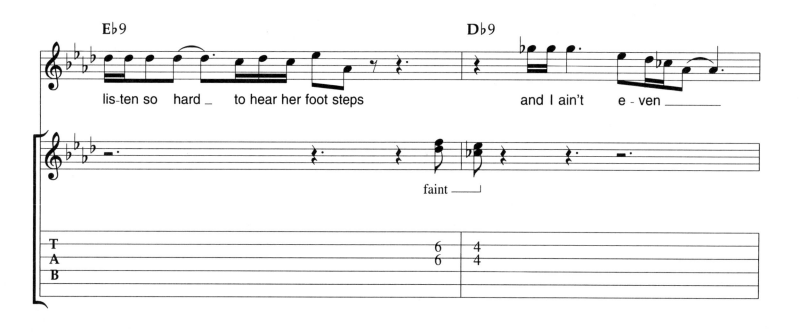

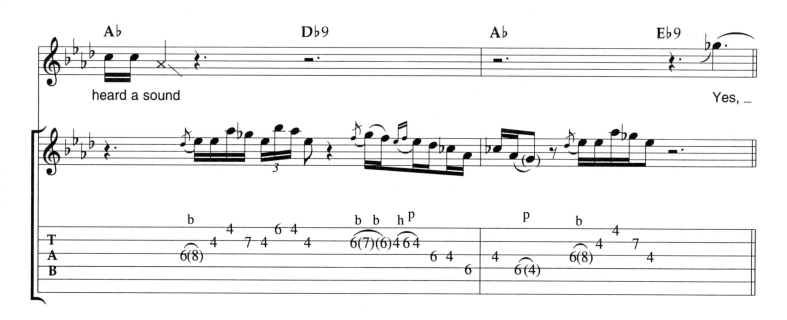

146

want my ba - by   Yes __ I want her by - my side

Well __ if she don't come home

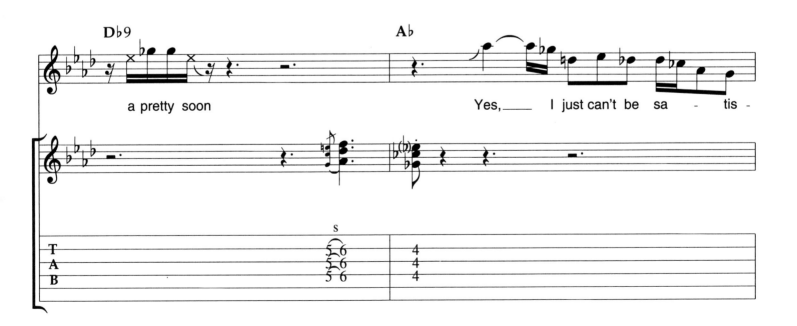

a pretty soon   Yes, __ I just can't be sa - tis -

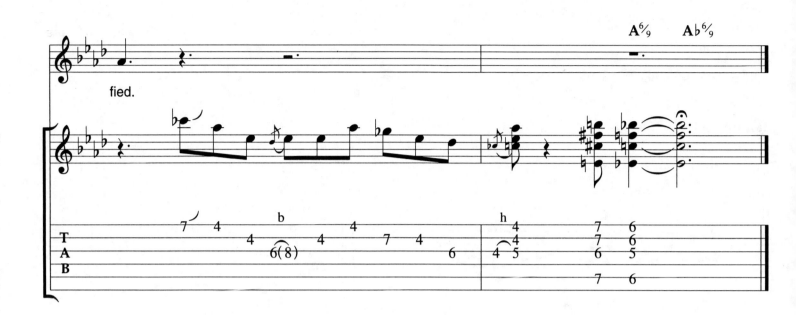

TUFF ENUFF

Transcribed Off The Recording by The Fabulous Thunderbirds on the Epic CD "The Fabulous Thunderbirds - Greatest Hits"

Guitar Tablature Transcription
by
Billy Simms

Three Guitars: Standard Tuning

⑥ = E   ④ = D   ② = B
⑤ = A   ③ = G   ① = E

Words and Music by
Kim Wilson

Medium Rock Groove

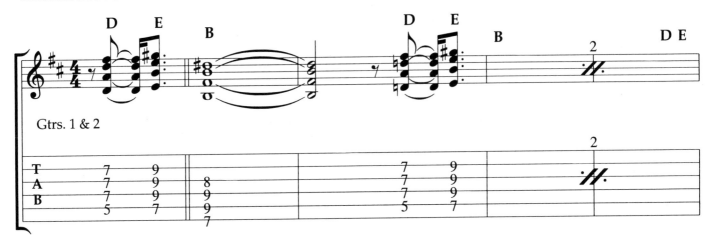

1. I would walk ten miles on my hands and knees.
2.3. & 4. (see additional lyrics)

Ain't no doubt a-bout it ba-by it's you I aim to please.___ I'd

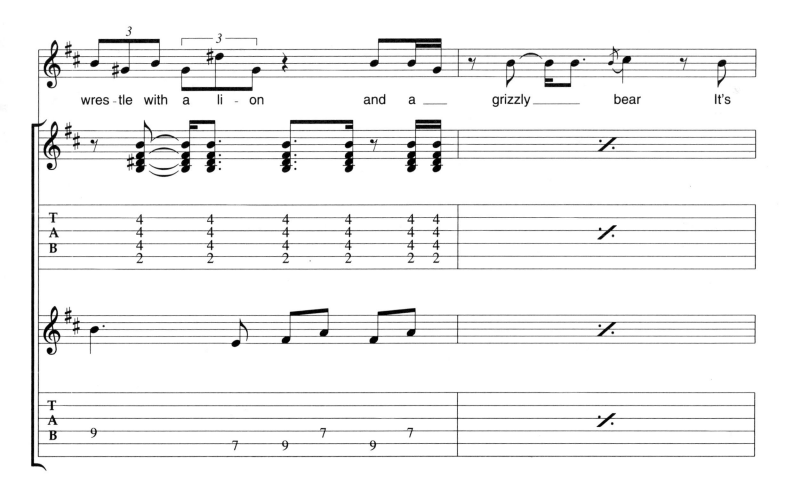

wres -tle with a li - on   and a ___   grizzly ____ bear   It's

To Coda ⊕

my   life ba - by but ___   I ___ don't care. Ain't __ that

(Chorus)

Tuff E - nuff   Ain't_ that Tuff E - nuff_   Aint _ that

Gtr. 1

Gtr. 2

Gtr. 3

* Strike string while turning volume knob up from the "0" position with Pinky.

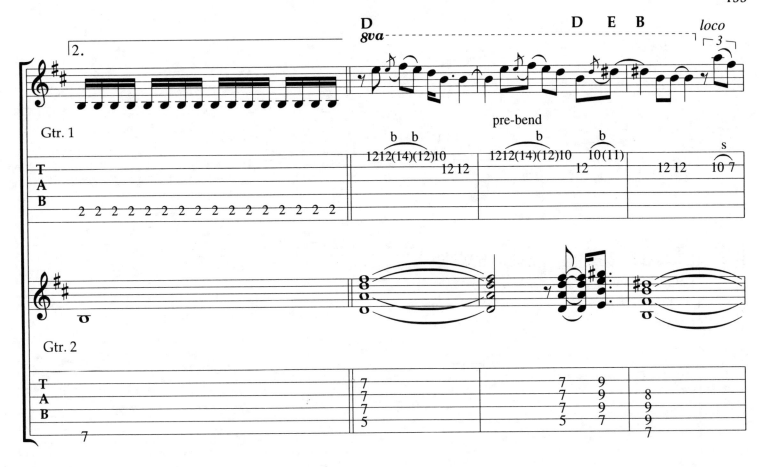

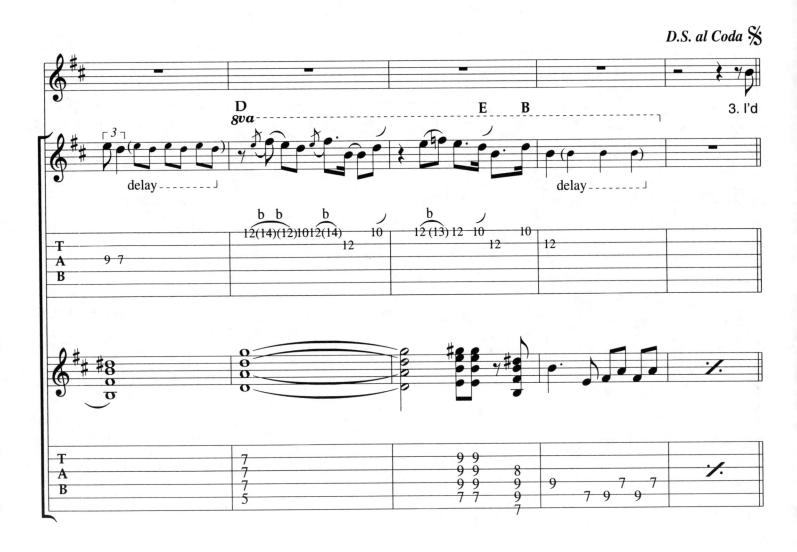

Coda

gtrs. 1, 2 & 3 repeat pattern of Chorus.

Ain't that Tuff E - nuff?   Ain't that Tuff E - nuff?   Ain't that

(fade out)

Tuff E - nuff?   Ain't that Tuff E - nuff?   Ain't that

Gtr. 1

Gtr. 2

Gtr. 3

Additional Lyrics

2. For you baby, I would swim the sea.
   Nothin' I'd do for you that's too tuff for me.
   I'd put out a burning building with a shovel and dirt,
   And not even worry about getting hurt.

3. I'd work twenty-four hours, seven days a week
   Just so I could come home and kiss your cheek.
   I love you in the morning and I love you at noon.
   I love you in the night take you to the moon.

4. I'd lay in a pile of burning money that I've earned
   And not even worry about getting burned.
   I'd climb the Empire State [Building], fight Muhammad Ali
   Just to have you, baby, close to me.